*Also by Ed W. McBee:*

**A Twisting Journey Continues**
*Northern Oregon Backroads Guide to the PCT
from Willamette Pass to the Bridge of the Gods*
Two Hats Publishing, 2020

# A Twisting Journey
## Southern Oregon Backroads Guide to the PCT

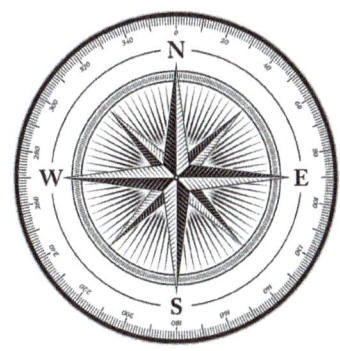

*from California to Willamette Pass*

# Ed W. McBee

Two Hats Publishing
Jacksonville, Oregon

Copyright © 2020 Ed W. McBee
All rights reserved

Photographs and maps by the author

**www.OregonBackroads.com**

Published by Two Hats Publishing LLC
Jacksonville, Oregon

ISBN 978-0-9904340-2-3

Minor Updates August 2023

This book contains images and text protected under International and Federal Copyright Laws and Treaties. No part of this publication, except for brief quotes in printed reviews, may be reproduced, stored in a retrieval system, or transmitted in any form or by any means, electronic, mechanical, photocopying, recording, or otherwise without prior written permission from the author.

The author, publisher and producers of this book are not responsible for injuries or accidents sustained by readers who follow activities described in this book. All maps and descriptions contained within this book are subject to change and should be used alongside maps issued by the Forest Service referenced in the book.

Book design by Lucky Valley Press
Jacksonville, Oregon
www.luckyvalleypress.com

Printed on acid-free paper

# CONTENTS

**INTRODUCTION**   1

## REGION ONE   19
### City of Jacksonville to Oregon Highway 66
Jacksonville, Ruch, Star Ranger Station, McKee Bridge, Jackson Park, Silver Fork Gap, Donomore Meadows, California state line, Jackson Gap, Wrangle Gap, Siskiyou Gap, Meridian Overlook, Mount Ashland Ski and Summit Roads, Interstate 5.

## REGION TWO   65
### City of Ashland to the town of Fort Klamath
Ashland, Emigrant Lake, Greensprings Summit, Hyatt Lake, Griffin Pass, Lake of the Woods, Great Meadow, Rocky Point, Upper Klamath Nat. Wildlife Refuge, Upper Klamath Lake.

## REGION THREE   103
### Town of Fort Klamath to Lemolo Lake
Fort Klamath Town, Historic Fort Klamath, Wood River, Crater Lake National Park, Pinnacles, Cloud Cap Overlook, Mount Scott, Diamond Lake, nearby waterfalls.

## REGION FOUR   143
### Lemolo Lake to Willamette Pass
Lemolo Lake area, waterfalls, Linda Lake, Timpanogas Lake, Summit Lake, Emigrant Pass, Crescent Lake, Crescent Lake Junction, Odell Lake, Willamette Pass.

**GENERAL INDEX**   187

**ROAD AND HIGHWAY INDEX**   194

# MAPS

## The Pacific Crest Trail in Southern Oregon     8

## Region One - City of Jacksonville to Oregon Highway 66

    **Map R1.1** Jacksonville to Interstate 5     20

    **Map R1.2** Silver Fork Gap area to Wrangle Gap     39

    **Map R1.3** Wrangle Gap to Ashland and Emigrant Lake     44

## Region Two - City of Ashland to the town of Fort Klamath

    **Map R2.1** City of Ashland to Highway 140     66

    **Map R2.2** Greensprings Summit Area     76

    **Map R2.3** Lake of the Woods to Crystal Springs     90

## Region Three - Town of Fort Klamath to Lemolo Lake

    **Map R3.1** Town of Fort Klamath to Crater Lake     104

    **Map R3.2** Crater Lake National Park     115

    **Map R3.3** Diamond Lake     129

## Region Four - Lemolo Lake to Willamette Pass

    **Map R4.1** Lemolo Lake to Willamette Pass     144

    **Map R4.2** Lemolo Lake Area     148

    **Map R4.3** Lemolo area to Timpanogas Lake     157

    **Map R4.4** Windigo Pass Area     159

    **Map R4.5** Timpanogas to Willamette Pass     165

### *Choices*
Life—and backroads guides—are twisting paths filled with choices.
Ketchup? Mustard? NO condiments at all?
Turn left, turn right; your senses will tell you what to do.
Sometimes your heart needs to do things without the brain's permission.
So at the next fork in your road, take it!

## *A Journey Calls*

    Exploring places in a timeless land,
Walking through mountains born of fire and formed by ice,
    I meet travelers along the way.
Learning the secrets of their
Beautiful world does brighten the day.
    Awakening is my reward for taking this Journey.
    With my eyes wide open,
I truly love this place called Oregon.

There are places and things we've not seen 'afore,
And before we're gone, shall we explore?

# Introduction

> *"The initial mystery that attends any journey is the question: How did the traveler reach his starting point in the first place?"*
> - Louise Bogan, American Poet Laureate

So there we were, rear wheel balanced on the edge of a serious precipice. On the CD player Bob Marley crooned, "Don't worry...'bout a thing... 'cause every little things...gonna be alright." Bob's prophetic words were eventually proven right but I wasn't convinced at the moment. My own fault, I suppose for trusting a Forest Service visitor's map.

A half hour before this we were at a six way intersection, high in the mountains of Oregon. My map showed this as a three way intersection. Discovering that signs marking any of these various road options were either missing or SUBAR (Shot Up Beyond All Recognition), I stopped. Licking my left index finger for luck, I consulted the runes and the aforementioned map, then took the road that seemed to lead in the right direction.

It was quickly apparent that this road was about to end when the tree branches reached their fingers closer to the paintwork. Weeds started to appear between the wheel tracks. I instinctively looked for a place to turn this circus around, but no such luck. The road ended abruptly at a washout.

Dang. It was time to see if I was born with the backup gene or not. Employing my innate, manly ability to fool myself, I turned up the music and shifted 'er into "R." Carefully, we edged down the mountain backwards as Bob sang on.

Brio, the well-traveled cowdog, hung his head out the window and woofed his concern as the road began to crumble away. Heeding his warning, I incrementally turned the steering wheel and so adjusted our trajectory to safely deliver us to a turnaround.

Man, I really hate backing up.

My goal was to drive the backroads of Oregon from California to Washington, avoiding the clutter of Interstate 5. Sounds easy enough, right? Shadowing the PCT (Pacific Crest Trail), I wanted to learn more about this amazing state of Oregon I now called home. Exploring a backroads version of the Pacific Crest Trail was the plan; wandering around a maze of unmarked logging roads wasn't what I had in mind. "Must be a better way than this," I muttered to the cowdog. He woofed in agreement. And so this guide began.

## Lessons Learned Growing Up in Kansas

OK, let's back this story up a lot of years. My family traveled extensively in the United States as I was growing up in Kansas and I eventually traveled to all 50 states. I have fond memories of fighting with my big sister in the backseat of the family station wagon (she started it) as we traveled across North America. A trip to the New York World's Fair in 1964 was my first memory of taking over the map and directing the family from our home in Kansas to New York City.

Dad was a map guy and always wanted to take the "scenic route" following the backroads where it was feasible and I was his willing accomplice. Mom was game as long as we didn't encounter any mountains and when we did, she would (half seriously) threaten to get out of the car and walk the rest of the way. Fortunately, Dad never gave in to the temptation to leave her in the Appalachians and we all moved forward together.

I belonged to the Boy Scouts, Troop 606 in Wichita (go Roadrunner Patrol!). Our troop was very active and we did some kind of monthly outdoor activity come rain, shine, or January. I had the opportunity to hike and camp in the Rocky Mountains of Colorado and northern New Mexico with the Scouts.

As a kid from Kansas I was bowled over by the sheer scale of the Rocky Mountain landscape. When examined up close, the sun splashed canyons and peaks revealed the grandeur of nature's beauty. Meandering trout streams beckoned us upwards to explore and camp beneath the cloak of moonless nights with the Milky Way arching impossibly above us.

If magic exists in this infinite universe it can surely be found there, in those rocky and wild places closest to the sky. Looking at the oversized landscape of the American west it seemed like an endless playground for a scrawny kid from the plains. Even today (more than 5 decades later) when I find myself in the mountains, I feel that Zen of sun-washed high country and big skies, a place of many possibilities. The lessons of self-reliance were great experience for a 13–14 year old, nerdy kid from Kansas. The confidence I gained with skills of backcountry navigation and outdoor living are things I've used all of my life.

*After the family moved from the plains of Kansas to a growing town on Puget Sound, a nerdy kid from the flatlands with a bad haircut became an Olympic View "Pirate." Yarghhh....*

## Toto, I don't think we're in Kansas anymore.

When I was 14 my parents moved the family from Kansas to the town of Mukilteo in Washington State. Dad worked for Boeing and was involved with the production and roll-out of the first 747 jetliner.

We were transported from the flatlands of Kansas to a home with a view of Puget Sound, surrounded by big trees, snow-capped mountains and the smell of salt water. That winter, my older sister and I learned to snow-ski at Stevens Pass, in the Cascades Mountains east of our new home. Definitely not in Kansas anymore…

After arriving in Washington I briefly joined a Scout troop based in Everett and found myself in the mountains again. One of the troop's volunteer projects was working on a section of existing trail near Stevens Pass that would eventually become part of the Pacific Crest

Trail (PCT). We spent a beautiful fall day in the High Cascades armed with Pulaskis, shovels and crowbars carving an improvement on this small section of trail.

Suddenly, I found myself arriving at the enlightened age of 15. From this lofty pinnacle, I decided the words "cool" and "Boy Scouts" didn't go together. With my interests shifting away from mountain scenery and more towards cars and a cute red-haired girl who thought Khaki green wasn't a proper color for me, the Scouts and I took different paths.

But this concept of a high country trail following the Pacific Divide continued to intrigue me. In 1969 I entertained the thought that someday I would backpack the completed Pacific Crest Trail. I hate to use this word but…Wow. To strap your home on your back and explore your way from Mexico to Canada would truly be a worthy goal. Some hardy souls even do it in one season. I've seen claims that fewer people have thru hiked the PCT in one season than have climbed Mount Everest. By Google's estimate, as of January 2023 about 6,338 individuals have summited Mount Everest.

Since the PCT crosses through three states and involves many moving parts over months of hiking, numbers of those successfully completing the trail are unreliable. The number of permitted hikers has increased steadily for several years, probably increasing the annual number of successful hikers.

### Update: August 2023

The effects of the COVID pandemic are still being reckoned with. The 2020 season saw a vast decrease in the number of hikers on the trail. The number of hikers on the trail in 2020 is unknown but had to be tiny compared to previous years. The good news for the PCT was a season of rejuvenation for areas normally impacted by hordes of hikers.

2023 has presented those who would challenge the trail with new obstacles. The unprecedented winter of 2022-23 delivered record amounts of snow to the Sierra with the southern part of the range seeing over 500% of the normal yearly average.

The allure of the PCT continues. Each season, adventurers are faced with new problems to solve and each year I'm amazed at the toughness and resiliency of those otherwise ordinary people who chose to take it on.

*The author backpacking in the lush Washington Cascades circa 1986. Before cell phones were invented, a huge pack, cotton clothing and a paper map was the way we rolled back in the old days.*

# The Pacific Crest Trail

The Pacific Crest National Scenic Trail (PCT) is a north/south foot trail (also open to hoofed travel) connecting Mexico to Canada through the states of California, Oregon and Washington.

Oilman and western outdoor enthusiast **Clinton C. Clarke** stands out as an early advocate for the trail. Envisioning the border-to-border trail "traversing the best scenic areas and maintaining an absolute wilderness character," Clarke recommended linking existing mountain trails in the three western states to form the PCT.

Clarke marshaled the resources of the Boy Scouts and the YMCA and over a period of four years (1935–1938), much of the trail was explored with a feasible route established. Following years of lobbying, the National Trail Systems Act was passed by Congress and signed into law on October 2, 1968.

The next two decades saw nearly 1,000 miles of new trail constructed by an army of volunteers cooperating with a bevy of public land management agencies, the Pacific Crest Trail Association (PCTA) and many other organizations.

From the Mexican border to the Oregon state line the PCT traverses nearly 1,700 miles of California. Oregon's section is a mere 460 miles and probably the easiest in terms of elevation change and ruggedness. From the trail's low point on the Columbia River, north to the Canadian border it's about another 500 (often rainy) trail miles through the lush Washington Cascades.

Spanning (roughly) 2,650 trail-miles and winding through some of the most rugged and wildly beautiful country remaining in the lower 48 states, today's PCT was officially completed in 1993.

The **"Crest" (not coast)** part of the PCT designation means that the trail strives to follow the high country divide of river waters that flow west and directly into the Pacific Ocean from those that flow east into the Great Basin and the Gulf of California in the southern part of the region.

The Pacific Crest Trail reaches its high point at Forrester Pass in California's Sierra Nevada Mountains. Forrester Pass along the PCT near Mount Whitney tops out at a lung-busting 13,153 feet.

In Oregon the "Skyline Trail" was an existing trail prior to the PCT and traversed the High Cascades from Mount Hood to Crater Lake and points south. Parts of the original trail still exist, some sections are paved over by modern roads and other sections became part of Oregon's section of the PCT. The PCT continues to evolve with the PCTA leading the way in efforts to sustain the quality of one of Earth's premier long-distance hiking trails.

*Travel nurse in the real world, Lindsey Clairmont embarks on an adventure. Starting at the Mexican border, the Pacific Crest Trail traverses some of the wildest country left in the lower 48 states, challenging travelers with rugged terrain and extreme weather. Note the mileage to Canada, 2,650 miles*

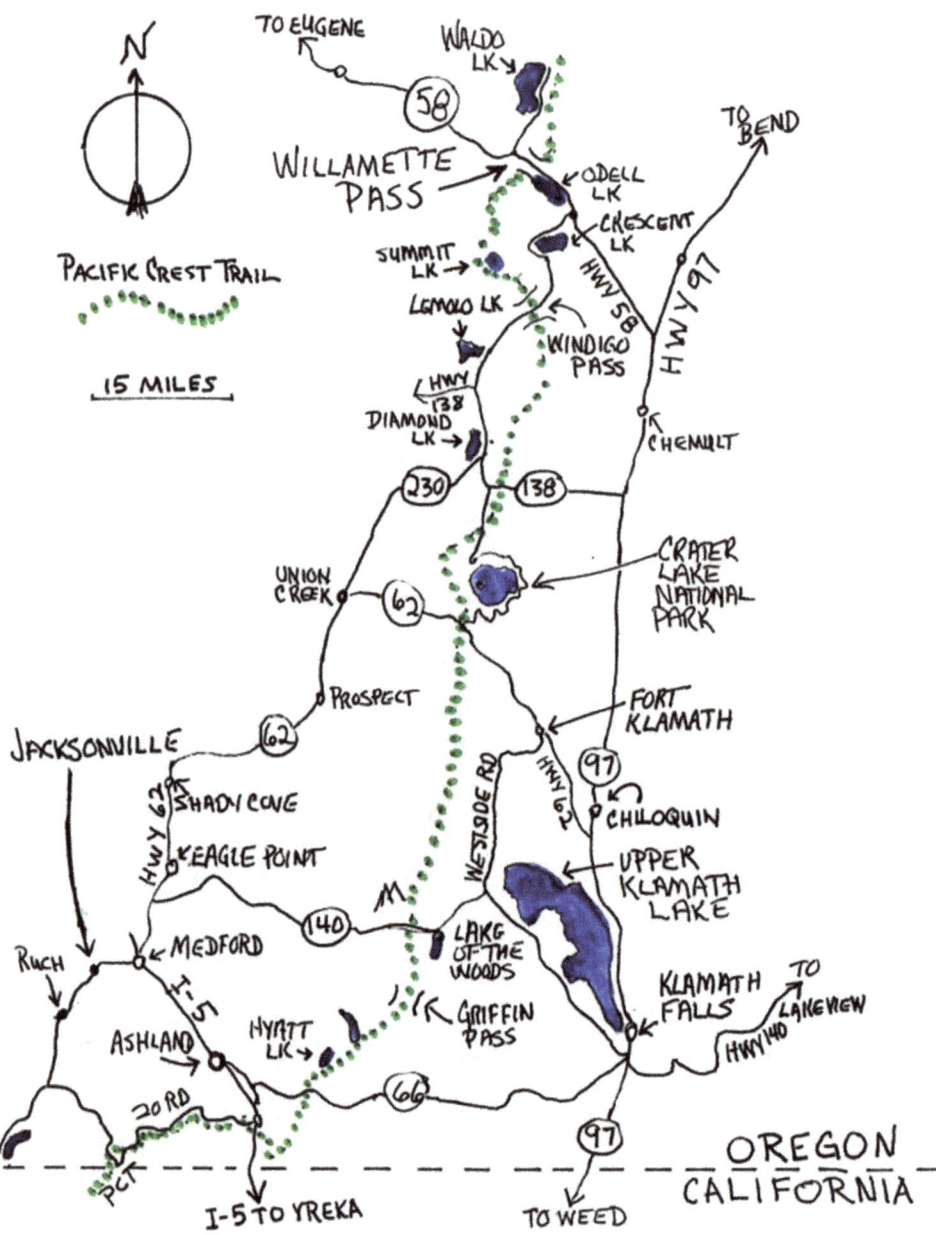

## The Pacific Crest Trail in Southern Oregon

The Pacific Crest Trail heads east after entering Oregon. Note that the trail crosses the state line well to the west of Interstate 5.

The road route description begins in Jacksonville and ends at Willamette Pass. Some of the smaller roads described in A Twisting Journey are not shown on this large scale map.

## Fast Forward to Little Disappointments

OK, back to the present. I'm thankful that I've lived in the beautiful Pacific Northwest (Washington, Alaska, and now Oregon) for more than 50 years. I've been fortunate to have the time and health to explore on foot vast areas of pristine backcountry in the Pacific Northwest. I've hiked long stretches of the Pacific Crest Trail in Washington, Oregon, and California, but I've resigned myself to the fact that I'll never hike the PCT from end to end in one season (or probably one lifetime). I admit it's true that life is full of little disappointments, but I'm lucky that mine has also been filled with many joys. Yes I'm older now and the knees do creak, but I'm not hanging up the hiking and camping gear yet. I still crave time in the mountains and enjoy them in all seasons.

Sure I use two hiking poles now but the sweet rush of wind through the mountain treetops still sings to me. Given the choice, I'll take the "scenic route" every time, (thanks for the genes, Dad). Of course now, instead of hoisting the butt-kicking 60lb pack with our home and food for a week on board, we're much more inclined to go camping with the big tent, folding cots, ice chest loaded with good food and drink, the dogs, etc. In other words, we try to travel lightly with the practical car camping outfit.

*Day-hiking near Sisters. If the surrounding area is interesting we can easily provision base camp with several days of supplies and day-hike from there. It's easy to break camp and move on if the wind blows us another way.*

Introduction

## The Journey Begins

After moving to Southwestern Oregon in 2002 I started to explore my new high country backyard. Looking at the local map to see the direction the Pacific Crest Trail takes as it enters Oregon from California, I noted an interesting road route that closely follows the trail as it travels east across the crest of the Siskiyou Mountains.

My first tentative trip into these mountains whetted my appetite for more. In my new backyard, the Pacific Crest Trail winds its way through the Siskiyou Range and a series of 7,000-foot-plus peaks as it heads east towards its connection with the upstart Cascade Mountains.

## The Lay of the Land

Oregon has always been a difficult place to get around in. Because of the rather orderly north/south nature of the Cascade Mountains, east/west travelers, will be confronted with this natural barrier. Several passes (low spots) present themselves to the traveler. In the Cascades, these natural east/west trails were well established foot paths for thousands of years before Europeans arrived on the scene.

In sharp contrast to the ordered nature of the Cascades, the tangled geography of the Klamath and Siskiyou Mountains of Southwestern Oregon makes travel in any direction especially tough. The Siskiyou Range is part of the geologically diverse Klamath Mountains of southern Oregon and northern California.

The Siskiyous are a rarity in North American geography with most mountains (like the Cascades) lying along a north/south axis. The Siskiyous run basically east/west connecting with the geologically young Southern Oregon Cascades near Ashland and the ancient Klamath Mountains to the west. This jumbled heap of mountainous terrain has been appropriately called the **"Klamath Knot"** and the connection provides for an incredibly rich biological and geological diversity.

## The Scenic Route

Some time ago I started thinking about traveling the length of Oregon. Shadowing the Pacific Crest Trail I would honor Dad and seek out the "scenic route." Traveling the backroads and staying in the high country would be my mantra. Keeping a journal along the way would be part of the fun too.

Avoiding the freeways and following the PCT from the point where it enters Oregon from the south (just like thru hikers on the PCT do) all the way to the Columbia River and Washington State in the north would be my ultimate goal.

Of course the "research" involved in exploring a road trip version of the PCT would mean I would have an excuse for doing some of the things I love best, kicking around the mountains and backroads of the American West. Dang...I'm a lucky guy!

### Don't Forget the Floater

If you have a small boat, a car topper or inflatable, opportunities abound for floating adventures. The canoe/kayak trail along the northwestern shore of Upper Klamath Lake is unique and primal.

The entire route passes by many lakes of significant size and several major streams. Even the first section through the Siskiyous has choice water features on both ends; the Applegate River and Emigrant Lake.

Ollalie Lake Scenic Area and other Regions north of Willamette Pass described in this book's companion, ***A Twisting Journey Continues: Northern Oregon Backroads Guide to the PCT,*** stand out among many great places to explore for adventurous paddlers or those who just want to enjoy high country sun, Earth, and water. And of course there are many hiking and camping opportunities along the way as well!

Both books in this series feature an amazing assortment of glacier carved alpine lakes and streams covering Oregon's crest country, many of them out-of-the-way gems.

Available at **http://www.oregonbackroads.com/** or independent booksellers near you.

## How to use this guide

### This guide is designed to be a supplement to your maps

Anyone who has traveled the backroads of Oregon can tell you what a challenge it can be. Many maps lack detail and the traveler quickly learns after leaving the pavement that the confusing maze of roads in the real world can be different than what a map shows.

Maps already on your smartphone can be useful but may not show critical details, don't rely on them alone. Paper maps last for years without charging the battery once. I once dropped a map off a 200 foot cliff and it still worked! So paper maps are super tough, too.

The Guide provides maps to help travelers along the general route and through key intersections. These maps are arranged starting with the Region number followed by the map number. "R" stands for Region.

> For example: **Map R2.1** refers to Region Two, map 1, the first map in Region Two.
>
> **Map R3.3** refers to Region Three, map 3.

New roads are added and old roads decommissioned. Attempts at signage over time come and go. Signs are sometimes flat out lies, missing or SUBAR (Shot Up Beyond All Recognition ). Some key intersections and general routes for each region are sketched out for clarity but take a map, too! As any good guide should be, this is definitely a work in progress. I have attempted to be as accurate as possible but know my efforts fall well short of perfection. I would ask the readers and users of this work to contact me with suggestions and corrections at ewmcb40@gmail. com

## Be Prepared! *(Wisdom from an old Boy Scout)*

**A word about safety and etiquette when traveling the back roads:**

**Consider the season and the weather** when planning a trip in the high country.

**Inquire locally** before traveling through snow country. Contact local Ranger Stations for information on local road conditions. Some storms can dump several feet of snow in a single blast and then, the weather may turn dry and sunny for weeks at a time. It's not unusual to see several feet of snow on the ground at any time in the late fall through early spring at high elevations in the Siskiyous and Cascades. It also hasn't been unusual in some recent years to see nothing on the ground in January followed by heavy snows through the spring months.

**Pay attention to the weather** and you'll sometimes find the most beautiful days in the mountains can be in January or February. This is especially true when the typical wintertime high pressure temperature inversions trap colder air and pollutants in the valleys below, leaving the higher terrain sunny and warm.

**Be careful with fire!**
Things can be critically dry in the mountains of Oregon during the summer and fall. A bucket and shovel are a good idea. Don't ignore fire restrictions and only start campfires in existing fire rings.

**Practice good etiquette.**
Traveling as lightly as possible across the land should be our goal. This means leaving a minimum footprint. Much of this route is through high country with thin soils and short growing seasons. Avoid driving off established roads and respect wetlands. Please be sure to pick up your own trash and pitch in to pick up after those less considerate.

**Fill your gas tank where you can!**
Just do it. Plan to use more fuel per mile on back roads. Your vehicle works at consistently lower gears because you're at altitude and going slower. When traveling off the beaten path, gas stations and grocery stores can be few and far between. A full gas tank is peace of mind, right?

**Allow extra time.**
Create the opportunity to stop and smell the wildflowers. Most regional routes described in this book are less than one hundred miles and can be driven (rushed through) in less time than the Guide recommends. However, much of the way is along less than perfect roads so expect to travel more slowly.

**Obtain maps of the area.**
This guide references Forest Service maps found at your friendly Ranger Station, but look for maps online, too. Despite the paucity of cellphone coverage in many of the areas described in the Guide, very useful *apps for navigating while offline* are available for your smartphone. Once the desired maps are loaded on your device you are independent of the internet. Another useful map for paper map freaks is the *Oregon Road and Recreation Atlas* published by Benchmark Maps and available at your local outdoor goods retailer. This has the entire set of Oregon maps laid out in logical fashion with tons of useful general information.

**Blankets /Sleeping Bags/Warm Clothes.**
Yes even in the summer. The high country is, well...high and that means changeable weather and potential for cold temps any time of the year. Bring water and food one gallon per person /beast per day is a good idea.

## Other Items to Consider:

I'm assuming everyone has that thang called common sense, so there's no need to mention all this stuff, right?

First Aid Kit Flashlight and Batteries, Matches/Lighter/Candle, Knife Hatchet/Ax/Folding Saw, Spade Tip Shovel (the most useful shape for most purposes), Jumper Cables/Spare Ignition Key, Chains during snow season, Small Tarp and at least 50 feet of Stout Rope, Sun Block, Insect Repellant, Toilet Paper, Folding Chairs (for bird watching bulls*ing, and beer drinking)?

I didn't think so...

Do you need all this stuff? Probably not, but just like flood insurance, that day when the water started rushing into your house, it's all worth it. I keep most of these items in an extra-large duffel bag, ready to toss in the car.

## Bad Feelings

If you ever get one of these gut feelings, stop and listen to your visceral self. Don't freak out, assess your options. Turn back if you have serious doubts. Is the snow piling up and the hour getting late? Don't hesitate to turn around before the snow gets too deep to do so easily.

Certain all-wheel drive vehicles (like a Subaru Outback) have just enough clearance and traction to get your ass in serious trouble when it becomes high centered. Your big snarly SUV/pickup (like a Toyota Tundra) can often travel even further up the mountain before high centering, so let's not be smug, eh?

Sometimes though, trouble comes in other forms. For instance, is your spare tire inflated? I'm not even going to ask if you have a jack and tire wrench. Another good way to get yourself in trouble is relying on your GPS (Global Positioning System). Although these devices are becoming more sophisticated, some serious high profile mishaps involving lost families have forced manufacturers to be more careful with "shortcut directions."

Google maps supplied with most smart phones today are remarkably accurate on the larger scale, but don't glue your eyes to the little blue dot while you drive off the cliff, OK? Off the beaten path, your smartphone is definitely useful where you can get reception (or the battery isn't dead), but don't rely on that alone.

## Download offline map apps for your smart phone.

The best problem solving device you have is your brain. It's also the best tool for staying out of trouble to begin with. Pay attention and don't drop your keys in the river... 'nuff said?

**Hangin' out in Southern Oregon's Siskiyou Range**

*Most of the road routes described in A Twisting Journey do not require high clearance or four-wheel-drive vehicles when the weather's fine and the living's easy. Try to tread lightly in the high country, winters are long and growing seasons are short. Looking southeast, distant Mount Shasta is seen just above the upraised canopy window.*

# A few words about vehicles

Regions One and Four have short stretches of rough road, not advised for low clearance vehicles. The majority of this route can be done in any vehicle with a short wheelbase and reasonable clearance in good weather. Where clearance and traction are an issue, I have provided alternate routes for those of us who like our low ridin' rigs.

Of course traveling as lightly as possible has its virtues beyond better gas mileage and a shorter turning radius. A smaller passenger car (a Toyota Camry for reference) has greater range and overall leaves a smaller footprint on the land but may have clearance and traction issues on rougher roads. All of the paved roads and most of the gravel roads described in this guide are suited for this vehicle in good weather.

Other short wheelbase, two-wheel drive vehicles (let's call it a Ford Ranger pickup) can often go places where a passenger car can't. In the backcountry, clearance is usually more of an issue than traction in good weather.

The other vehicle in the mix is the new generation of midsize SUVs" with all-wheel drive. This type of vehicle is a nice compromise for clearance, maneuverability, gas mileage and traction.

Your big snarly/gas hoggy, four-wheel drive SUV or pickup (let's call it a Lincoln Navigator) has lots of room for the family and gear and has all the clearance and traction you'll probably ever need to ford a river or scale a mountain, but when was the last time you needed to do that? Needless to say, in good weather, none of the road descriptions contained within this guide are beyond the capabilities of such vehicles.

Explore, enjoy, and wave (at least lift your little finger off the steering wheel) to your fellow travelers!

> The freedom of the hills calls to me.
> And so I must go.
>
> *Ed W. McBee*

# Each Regional Description Begins With:

**Main Roads in Order of Travel:** With a description of each.

**Optional Roads and other Attractions:** More fun stuff.

**Pacific Crest Trail Access Points:** Self-explanatory, trailhead information is useful for day hikers, section hikers, and those supporting hikers. Trail miles on the PCT are included here.

**Route Description:** Provides a general description of the roads we'll be traveling plus clearance or traction issues and notes on seasonal closures.

**Maps of the Area:** Includes information for obtaining needed maps in person and apps online.

**Road Notes:** Mostly ramblings of an old dude from Kansas... also describes what to expect along the way including scenery, wildlife, history, restaurants/bars, groceries/gas, lodging, resorts/camping/fishing, hiking and more.

*Beaten but not bested. A wind battered white pine stands guard atop a ridge in the Siskiyou Range.*

*Manned lookouts are becoming increasingly rare as modern technology replaces human eyes to detect and report fires. The lookout atop the Siskiyou Mountains' Dutchman Peak is the last of the cupola style lookouts occasionally manned during the fire season. Accessible by road (4-wheel-drive recommended) or a short hike if the gate is closed.*

# Region One

## City of Jacksonville to Oregon Highway 66

*Wanna Go For a Ride?*

"And they was trying to get to heaven
In an electric car
And that car wheel slipped
On down the hill
Instead of going to heaven
They went to Jacksonville."
~ **Lyle Lovett**
*Since the Last Time*

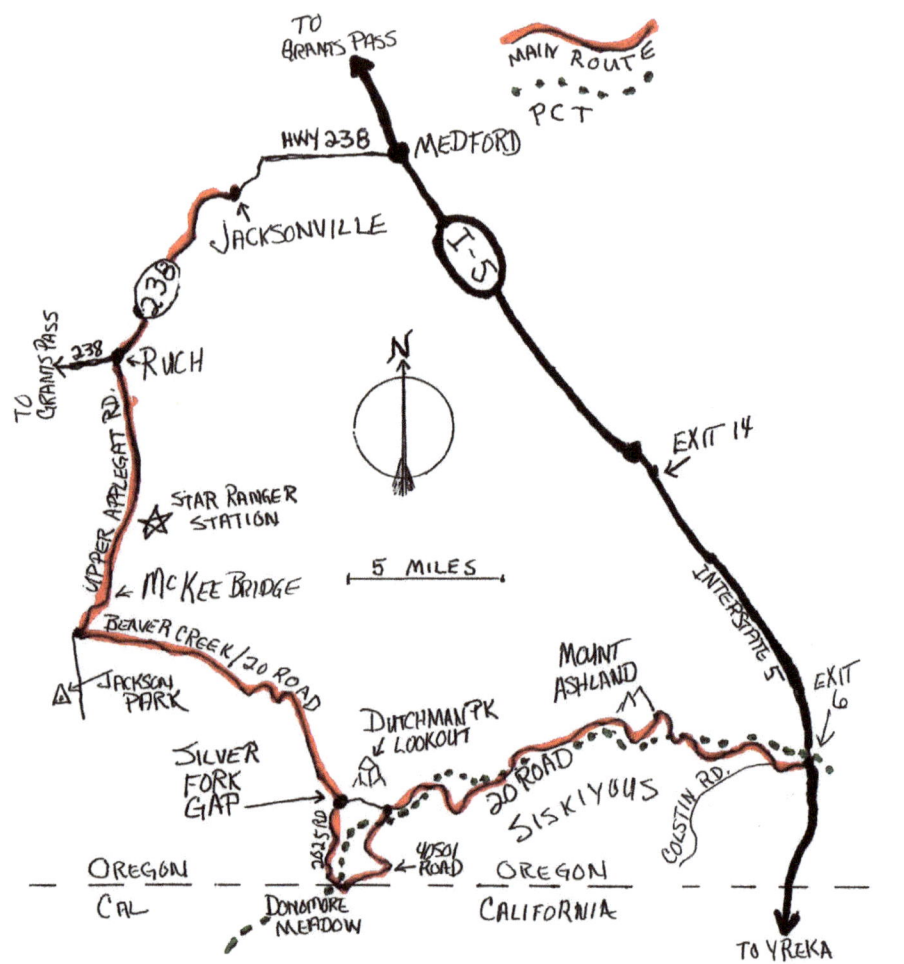

**Map R1.1 Jacksonville to Interstate 5**

*The inviting 20 Road is the star of the show in Region One. As it edges along the crest of the Siskiyous it presents travelers with plenty of great opportunities to explore on this verge of southern Oregon and northern California. With the Pacific Crest Trail winding above and below the road there are lots of places to jump on the PCT for a short hike or just take a walk in the woods.*

# REGION ONE MAIN ROADS IN ORDER OF TRAVEL

**Beginning in Jacksonville:**

**Highway 238**
Southwest from Jacksonville to Ruch.

**Upper Applegate Road**
South from Ruch to Beaver Creek Road.

**Beaver Creek Road**
Becomes Forest Road 20 where the pavement ends.

**Forest Road 20**
Wide and graveled with some stretches of washboards, takes us to Silver Fork Gap.

**Road 2025**
From the Gap this easy road meanders south to the PCT and the California state line.

**Road 40S01**
Narrow in places with some ruts, probably not advised for passenger cars.

**Back on the 20 Road**
Past Wrangle Gap, the 20 Road is rough for a few miles to Meridian Overlook. Not for passenger cars.

**Road 1151**
This is the Mount Ashland Ski Road.

**Old Highway 99**
Avoiding I-5, the old highway delivers us to Highway 66.

**Highway 66**
Turn left to go to Ashland or right to Greensprings Summit.

# Optional Roads and Other Attractions Described in Region One

**Road 800:**
The driveway from Jackson Gap to Dutchman Peak Lookout. If the gate is open, four wheel drive is recommended.

**Jackson County Park:**
Just south of the Beaver Creek intersection on the Upper Applegate River Road.

**Donomore Meadows:**
In California near the point where the PCT enters Oregon from California. A restored herder's cabin sits atop a knoll on the north side of the meadows.

**Mount Ashland Summit Road:**
Steep and narrow with amazing views, this road delivers us to the highest peak in the Siskiyous, a must see (forever) on a clear day.

## PCT ACCESS POINTS IN REGION ONE

The 20 Road parallels the PCT through the Siskiyous making the trail accessible at many points along the way. Of more specific interest to Section and Day-Hikers is the trail's entrance into Oregon from California and other access points closer to Interstate 5.

The PCT crosses I-5 near Siskiyou Summit at trail mile 1716.4. Many people assume that the PCT entering Oregon from California is routed closer to I-5 and that the trail enters Oregon near there, but as the crow flies, the PCT enters the state more than 16 miles west of I-5. **Pretty much in the middle of nowhere**.

The PCT crosses the middle of nowhere at the 2025 Road, trail mile 1,689.5, just 0.3 miles north of the Oregon/California state line trail register. The hike northbound (NOBO) from the state line to hiker friendly Callahan's Lodge (located on I-5) is about 27 miles. **Map R1.2**

Another popular access to the PCT for day-hikers is at Grouse Gap, just west of Mount Ashland along the 20 Road, Trail mile 1,705.7. **Map R1.3**

The next major road crossing of the PCT northbound (NOBO) after leaving I-5 is at Greensprings Summit, PCT mile 1,733, 16.3 trail miles north from I-5. **Map R2.1**

## City of Jacksonville

*Our exploration of Southern Oregon's section if the PCT begins in Jacksonville. After a series of devastating fires swept through town leveling the original wooden structures, much of downtown was rebuilt (by official government decree) with more fire resistant bricks.*

*The old Redmen's Hall, tattooed with advertising, is an impressive structure and has survived since the 1800's. On the corner the "Boomtown" business name echoes the gold rush that originally put the town on the map.*

I've driven (with care) my four-door Japanese sedan from Jacksonville to the point the Pacific Crest Trail enters Oregon from California many times with consequences no worse than a dusty car.

A short wheel-base, good brakes, and reasonable clearance will get you there and back in good weather. If your goal is the PCT trailhead, high clearance four-wheel drive vehicles allow more extensive exploration in the region but aren't necessary in warm, dry weather if you stick to the main roads.

The continuation of the road route past the PCT trailhead is not recommended for passenger cars.

> **Note:** Because of the high elevation along the Siskiyou Crest (over 7,000 feet in places), Forest Service Road 20 is typically closed by snow from late fall until early summer. Other state highways and paved roads described in Region One are plowed in the winter.
>
> Early in the hiking season and late in the fall the weather can get dicey. It's important to go prepared for severe weather during the fringes of the seasons.
>
> Traction devices like chains and 4-wheel drive should be included in your kit in the late fall and early winter. Pay attention to the weather forecast and bring warm clothes and blankets even in the summer. Think about bringing a spade tip shovel, at least 50 feet of stout line, food, and extra water for beasts and human critters, too.
>
> Check that your cell phone battery is juiced, the spare tire is fat, and the gas tank is full as you go forth fearlessly.
>
> Contact the Star Ranger Station at: 541-899-3800 (Mon-Fri) for up-to-date road information.

# REGION ONE ROUTE DESCRIPTION

Why begin in Jacksonville? Besides being an interesting town to explore, it's the last place to get gas. Also, if your goal is the Or/Cal state line of the PCT, you and your car will take less of a pounding traveling to that trail-crossing from Jacksonville than if you were to travel the 20 Road from Mount Ashland.

The roads from Jacksonville to the PCT trailhead on the OR/Cal state line are mostly paved with the last 11 miles graveled. Yeah, there are some bouncy washboards on the up/down hill sections but any car can do it.

Starting in Jacksonville, Oregon we'll travel west on Highway 238 to the town of Ruch.

We'll leave Highway 238 at Ruch and drive south on the Upper Applegate Road. Just past the historic McKee Covered Bridge, we'll turn east on the paved Beaver Creek Road.

Near where the pavement ends, the improved gravel road (with some ugly washboards along the uphill sections) becomes Forest Road 20 and gains altitude before arriving at Silver Fork Gap, elevation 6,364 feet.

From Silver Fork Gap we'll follow the easy, improved gravel 2025 Road about 4 miles south to the first road crossing for northbound hikers of the Pacific Crest Trail in Oregon.

Total mileage from Jacksonville to the PCT trailhead is about 30 miles, one-way. Allow about an hour and a half travel time.

From the PCT trailhead we'll head northeast on the nearby 40S01 Road, rejoining the 20 Road at Jackson Gap, elevation 7,027 feet.

The sometimes rugged 20 Road heads east from there and meets the pavement at Mount Ashland Ski Road before crossing (under) Interstate 5 and ending at State Highway 66.

# MAPS FOR REGION ONE

The recommended **Applegate and West Half of Ashland Ranger Districts Map** is an excellent map of the area we'll be exploring and is available at the Star Ranger Station.

You can also get the more general **Rogue River-Siskiyou National Forest Map** at the station or order either one online.

Some of the areas we'll be traveling through are sketchy when it comes to the 21st century version of a security blanket, cellphone coverage in other words. I'm old and crusty and cling to my ancient, misfolded paper maps while acknowledging some excellent downloadable maps available for your smartphones, I'll leave it up to the user which one works for you. Download them at home and once the maps are loaded onto your device you are independent of cell coverage.

Yes I'm so old **I remember when phones were just for calling people** (they also had a cord attaching them to a wall!) and if you tried to take a picture with it people would of locked you up.

Maps don't rely on the battery being charged or having cell towers nearby, so touché technology... Ha!

*Silvery Blue butterflies (glaucopsyche lygdamus) can sometimes be found in abundance in the high Siskiyou Mountains. Look for these striking flutterers near damp soils where adult males can be observed collecting the salts necessary for breeding.*

# ROAD NOTES FOR REGION ONE

## City of Jacksonville to Silver Fork Gap and the PCT

→ Allow 4-5 hours with stops.

→ Jacksonville is the last place for gas.

### Jacksonville  *Elevation 1,570 feet*

To a very large degree, Jacksonville owes its present-day charm to a series of disasters following the discovery of gold here in 1851. When word of the strike got out, a rush of miners from the gold fields in California descended on what was originally called Table Rock City.

The landscape was altered as hordes of hard rock miners at first cut away the hillsides by hand and with explosives, following the veins of gold-bearing ore.

Later they dug ditches and channeled water over miles, powering hydraulic cannons (called giants) to wash away millions of tons of rocks and soil to wrest the precious metal from the Earth.

After the Rogue Indian Wars of 1855-56, many of the Native American survivors that had lived in the area for thousands of years were rounded up and forced to leave their lands. A disaster for the environment and the native people as well.

The town gained some prominence as mining operations expanded in the area and at one time Jacksonville boasted of being the largest city in the Oregon Territory. Rapid growth and speculation led to haphazard construction of wooden structures and the inevitable series of disastrous fires which periodically leveled large sections of the town. Fire resistant bricks were used to build many of the surviving structures seen today in the historic district.

## The Wrong Side of the Tracks

The next disaster coincided with the playing out of gold deposits locally. Mines were closing and jobs disappearing a decade after the American Civil War. After the war, the United States embarked on a railroad building binge and a rail line connector to the transcontinental terminus in Sacramento, California was being constructed through western Oregon beginning in the early 1880s. Jacksonville was the county seat and economic hub of Southern Oregon at the time and it was assumed by many residents that the railroad would be routed along the old stage road that passed through that town. When the railroad routed its line through Medford and by-passed Jacksonville, the once thriving town began a rather precipitous decline as businesses and citizens gravitated towards Medford for jobs and business opportunities.

Jacksonville became the town that was literally "on the wrong side of the tracks." Many of the old brick buildings were allowed to fall into disuse with windows boarded over. "Jville" is where you lived if your financial options were limited. More tunnels were dug under the town during the Great Depression of the 1930s by hungry citizens looking for gold. Modern-day heavy trucks and construction equipment now periodically sink into old excavations. Post-World War II and the end of the Great Depression spurred a building boom nationwide creating logging jobs in the nearby Cascades and Siskiyous and mill work in the Rogue River Valley.

Still…Jacksonville lingered, yet to be 'discovered.' That is until a group of citizens organized in the late 1960s to save the remaining buildings in the governmental, residential and commercial districts.

Today, the "National Historic Landmark District" of Jacksonville, one of 18 or so designated historical landmarks in the state of Oregon, contains over 100 buildings of historic significance. 21st century Jacksonville is an attractive town of around 3,000 souls, nestled into the foothills of the Siskiyou Mountains.

The town hosts many festivals and events throughout the year with the signature event being the summertime musical festival. Officially known as the **Britt Musical Festival** but called "The Britt" by the locals, it's an outdoor event held on the grounds of founding father Peter Britt's homestead just above town. Spanning several weeks in the summer, the old Britt homestead is a great venue for the classical music portion of the festival featuring the Britt orchestra made up of musicians from around the world.

Walking from Illinois, Peter Britt arrived in Jacksonville in early 1852 as gold was being discovered and word of the strike was getting out. At first trying his hand at gold mining he soon turned to other enterprises like wine making and photography. Many of Britt's early photos of the area survive including the first pictures taken of Crater Lake.

Many renowned acts take to the outdoor stage during the Pop season. Look to **brittfest.org** for more information about performance schedules.

*Enterprising Jacksonville pioneer Peter Britt settled in Jacksonville in 1852. A trained portrait painter, Britt adopted the new technology of the time, photography. He experimented with varieties of grapes suited to the local climate and orchard plants, like pears and peaches. His first photo of Crater Lake was taken in 1874. This (oddly posed) statue of Mr. Britt currently scares children near the entrance to the Britt grounds. The yearly musical festival was named after Mr. Britt.*

The Jacksonville Barber Shop is comfortably furnished with many antique and vintage pieces, the barber calls it the "Museum of Barbarism." The barber shop is the oldest continuously operated business in Jacksonville and features a mural of the Applegate River and the high Siskiyous in the distance.

"Oysters and Ales" night at the Bella Union can draw a big crowd. Look for live music in the Saloon and fresh oysters on the patio during the shellfish season. Bring your sense of humor please...

Before leaving Jacksonville, take a walking tour of the downtown area to soak-up the ambiance of late 19th century architecture. The varied collection of restaurants, bars, and eclectic shops attracts crowds on a warm summer day. Traffic is stop-and-go with parking at a premium during Britt shows and other seasonal events; watch out for distracted drivers as you stroll about the narrow streets.

For more ambitious hikers there's a network of trails covering several miles through the foothills above town with interpretative signs marking the various mining sites and attractions along the route. The Chamber of Commerce kiosk next to the Post Office is a good source of local information with maps showing local walking trails including the nearby Forest Park and more miles of trails.

The **Bella Union Restaurant and Saloon** offers up "Oysters and Ales" during the September through April oyster season. Various regional breweries and distributors offer beer tastings and oysters are served fresh or on the grill. There's live music in the saloon and the "blowout" marking the end of oysters in April draws a big crowd.

Take a look at the ornate woodwork inside the **Boomtown Saloon** as you enjoy a full bar and extensive selection of northwest craft style beers. Located on the corner of California and 3rd Streets, the friendly watering hole features giant windows great for people-watching as you sip your brew; look for the shuffleboard table lining one wall.

It's easy to spend an afternoon exploring the interesting shops and businesses occupying the Historic District. Don't forget to take a peek inside the **Jacksonville Barber Shop**. The barber shop is the oldest, continuously operated business in town and has a variety of antique and vintage furnishings.

A wide selection of restaurants offers everything from good Mexican food to fine dining. For breakfast try the **Mustard Seed** located next to the old courthouse on 5th Street. The indoor seating area is limited with more space outside when the weather permits; the homemade soups are locally legendary. **Las Palmas** has a nice outdoor patio area and friendly service. Try their tasty shrimp enchiladas with a margarita on the rocks. The venerable **Jacksonville Inn** has a more formal dining room and a more in-formal bistro located near the old **United States Hotel**.

## Jacksonville to Ruch

From the corner of California and Oregon Streets in downtown Jacksonville, Highway 238 heads west and uphill as we leave Jacksonville behind and head towards the town of Ruch (pronounced *roosh*). The sign says it's 8 miles to Ruch but the mileage is actually closer to 7 miles to **our turn-off at Upper Applegate Road.**
The highway follows Jackson Creek at first; just out of town look for the parking area to the left marking the trailhead for the Britt Trails. The popular day-hiking trails here and above town are also named after Peter Britt.

The highway begins to trend southwest as we top Jacksonville Hill and enter the Applegate Valley. The road winds its way downhill as we pass through gorgeous farm and woodlands. Before arriving at Ruch, and looking to the left (south) we'll spot Woodrat Mountain marked by clearings along its upper slopes. These clearings are used as launching pads for paraglider pilots taking advantage of the local up-drafts. Pilots from around the world gather here to participate in annual competitions.

For information on the local gliding scene look online at **rvhpa.org**.

# The Town of Ruch  *Elevation 1,527 feet*

> **Note:** We'll leave Highway 238 at the town of Ruch and head south on the **Upper Applegate Road.**

Ruch is the commercial and residential center for this part of the gorgeous Applegate Valley. Along with a couple of small cafes and garden stores catering to the burgeoning number of cannabis farmers who have descended on the valley, there's a well-stocked grocery store with an extensive deli. You will also find a visitors center with information on the town, nearby recreational opportunities and the growing number of local wineries.

There are numerous local events and attractions held at various wineries located in the Applegate Valley growing region; a day's exploration would only begin to acquaint wine aficionados to the many tasting rooms available locally.

We're turning off the highway here, but Highway 238 continues west through town following the Applegate River several miles downstream and eventually arrives at the city of Grants Pass.

## From Ruch it's about 8.6 miles to the Beaver Creek intersection

The Upper Applegate River Road heads directly south as we leave Ruch, passing through residential neighborhoods before opening up to acres of vineyards adjacent to the tasting rooms of **Valley View Winery**. Stop in and meet the friendly staff while you sample the delicious local wines produced here. Some of the oldest vines in the Applegate Valley are contained within the neatly arranged vineyard; gaze across the valley from here at the steeply rising foothills of Southern Oregon's Siskiyou Range.

Shortly after leaving the grape yards the road crosses the Little Applegate River and then parallels its main fork as we travel further south. The scenery on display here is the essence of Southern Oregon's rural landscapes, mixing ranch and farm land with the sparkling waters of the Applegate River and distant snow-capped mountains of the Red Buttes Wilderness and the high Siskiyous. The river is renowned with steel headers targeting the metal heads during the winter season opener, January through March.

*The Valley View Winery's tasting room is located one mile south of Ruch along the Upper Applegate River Road. Stop in and sample the beautiful scenery and fine wines offered here. The outdoor deck offers sweeping views and the adjacent vineyard has some of the oldest vines in Southern Oregon.*

## Star Ranger Station and McKee Bridge

Before we reach McKee Bridge and our turn-off at the Beaver Creek Road, we arrive at the Star Ranger Station.

The ranger station sells an excellent map of the area we'll be exploring titled, *Applegate and West Half of the Ashland Ranger Districts*. The map is a highly detailed topo (1 inch = 2 miles) of the high Siskiyous and well worth the price. Grab yours now if you don't have it already.

Just inside the front door of the ranger station, a full sized stuffed mountain lion is on display. If you'd like to give Fido a thrill, put him on a leash and give him the tour; yes it's OK with the staff who seem to relish the look of the dog's reaction upon encountering the lion at eye level.

The station is open Monday through Friday, 541-899-3800. Or look for info online.

*The McKee Covered Bridge was constructed to move trucks laden with copper ore from the now abandoned Blue Ledge Mine. Closed to vehicular traffic, it makes a novel pedestrian crossing of the Upper Applegate River.*

## Beaver Creek Road Intersection

**Special Note!** Jackson Park and Campground is a pleasant spot on the Applegate River and lies just 1/2 mile south of the Beaver Creek intersection. To drive to the park stay on the Upper Applegate Road heading south and look for the entrance to your right. Located between the road and the cold clear Applegate River, the fee area has water, vault toilets and a day-use area.

This is a great place to look for water loving birds like ouzels and belted kingfishers. There is a beautiful gravel beach with plenty of shallow areas to splash around in the ice-cold river on hot summer days. The park and surrounding waters are popular with fishermen during the winter steelhead season. The campground is a bit tightly spaced with no hook-ups so this isn't the ideal place for giant motorhomes. For information and reservations call 541-899-9220 or look online at www.applegatelake.com

## Beaver Creek Road to Silver Fork Gap
*Elevation 1,670 feet at the turn-off*

**Note:** The Beaver Creek Road intersection is well signed pointing east towards Dutchman Peak Lookout and Mount Ashland. The road gains something like 4,700 feet elevation so let's get crackin'! We'll be on this road for 13.2 miles to our next turn at Silver Fork Gap.

The Beaver Creek Road starts out paved before the asphalt peters-out past the 5 mile mark. Officially becoming Forest Road 20 as it enters the Rogue River National Forest, the road is wide and well graveled but develops some washboards along the steeper grades.

Slow down and take it easy; you and your car will take less of a pounding. One of the major twists in the road ahead is labeled "Deadman's Curve" so be prepared for some steep grades and sharp corners. The road heads steadily up and southward, keep to the left and on the 20 Road at any major junctions you may encounter. Views to the south and west begin to open up past the 10 mile marker and the copper colored peaks of the Red Buttes Wilderness are visible in the distance. A little more than 13 miles after leaving the Beaver Creek intersection we arrive at the nicely named Silver Fork Gap.

*The aptly named Copper Butte stands out in the center of this shot. Part of California's Red Buttes Wilderness Area, the distinctive ridge line is visible from the 20 Road before we arrive at Silver Fork Gap.*

## Silver Fork Gap to the PCT
*Elevation 6,364 feet at the Gap*

> **Note:** We'll leave the 20 Road at Silver Fork Gap and drive south on the 2025 Road to the PCT trailhead.

This is a 6-way intersection so please take your time getting oriented before we proceed.

A "Gap" in this sense is a low spot or saddle in the Siskiyou Range.

The "Silver Fork" part refers not to tableware but to the Silver Fork branch of Elliot Creek which heads near here and flows into the Applegate River just above Applegate Lake Reservoir, about 10 miles (as the crow flies) to the west. Since we arrived on the 20 Road from the north we should be looking almost due south.

The road we want is the "main" road (bigger and obviously more traveled) **heading downhill** and southeast from this intersection, this is the 2025 Road.

> **Note!** The 2025 road sign was missing the first "2" as of summer 2023 so appeared to mark the road as the 025 Road.

Probably not signed correctly, it's the obvious choice for drivers heading south **(and again, downhill)**. The continuation of the 20 Road is probably marked and stays on the level. This is the "main" road to the left (east) through the trees and it goes to Jackson Gap, Dutchman Peak Lookout, and ultimately Mount Ashland and I-5. We'll hook up with the 20 Road later at Jackson Gap. The other three roads are secondary roads.

Leaving the intersection, the 2025 Road at first heads downhill and southeast from Silver Fork Gap; it's about **3.8 miles from the gap to the PCT trailhead.** The road in places has remnants of pavement mixed in with some minor potholes as it contours the flanks of Observation Peak heading south.

After leveling out, the 2025 Road winds its way through mixed alpine forest and meadowlands before we arrive at the first crossing of the **Pacific Crest Trail,** elevation 6,197 feet. The universal PCT signs were replaced here in 2019 and make the trail crossing easier to spot but no flashing lights or ceremony here.

## PCT Trailhead

Park here and lace your boots on if you want to stroll down the trail to the actual California state line, it's about a 0.3 mile walk from the road to the hiker's registration box. Here again, not a lot of fanfare but if you're a thru-hiker on the PCT and after many weeks of hiking almost 1,700 miles through California from Mexico, you are celebrating the fact you are nearly 2/3 of the way to Canada AND... you're in a new state!

The metal box containing the hiker's information (along with a trove of offerings) and the sign marking the state line and the mileages to Canada and Mexico are the only monuments to this invisible line.

For those who choose to hike the length of Oregon starting from the south, mark this as the beginning of your journey.

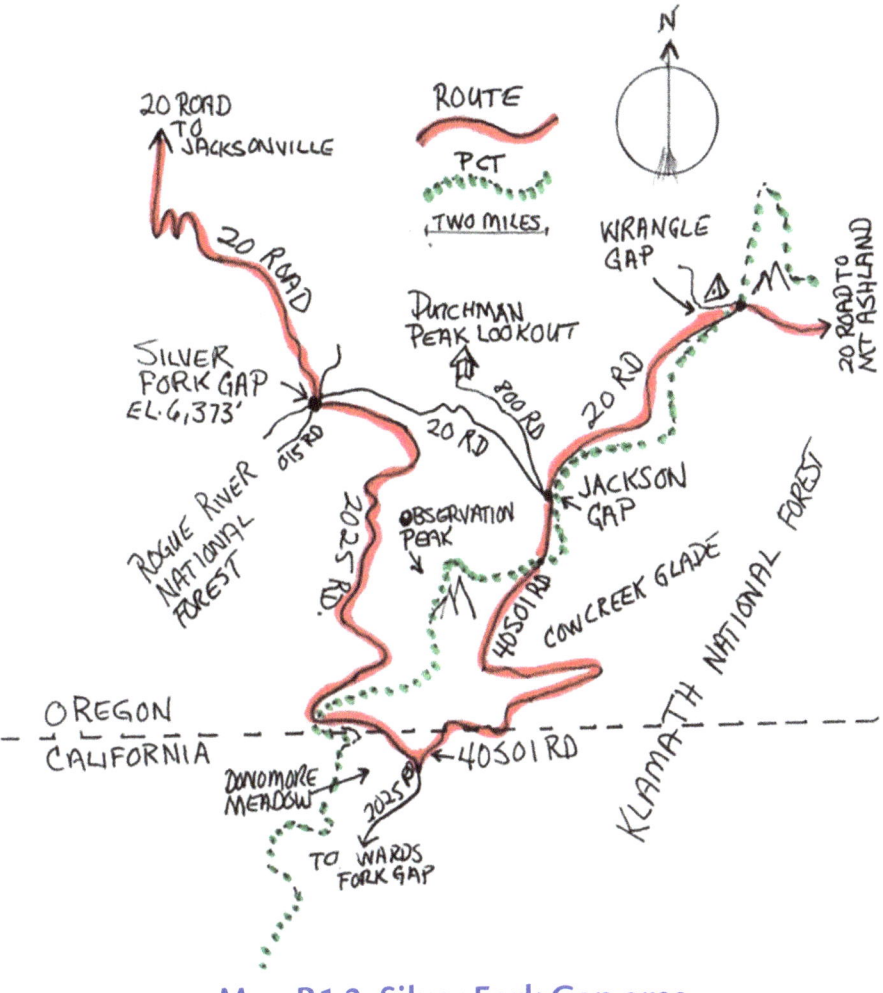

Map R1.2  Silver Fork Gap area
and the route to Wrangle Gap

## Silver Fork Gap, Dutchman Peak and Jackson Gap

Lots of cool stuff to explore in this out-of-the-way edge of Oregon and northern California. Donomore Meadow is in California near where the PCT enters Oregon and worth a tour of the old herder's cabin.

Dutchman Peak is accessible by four-wheel drive vehicles when the gate is open, otherwise it's a short walk to the look-out. Jackson Gap is a major crossroad in the high Siskiyous. Cow Creek Glade is a designated botanical area of interest.

**Hikers on the PCT!** *Celebrations are heartfelt for thru hikers from around the world. To reach the Oregon/Cal state line, NOBO hikers (northbound) have walked a minimum of 1,689 trail miles from the Mexican Border. Trail Angels from the Jacksonville area are known to occasionally greet hikers as they enter Oregon after many weeks in California and a long grind up the hot and dry Southern Siskiyous from the Klamath River.*

### Pacific Crest Trail to the 40S01 Road intersection

Our next turn will be left (east) at the 40S01 Road.

> **Note:** If your goal was to discover the beginning of Oregon's section of the PCT and you want to get to Ashland and I-5 from the trailhead, you might consider going back through Jacksonville rather than driving the continuation described from here. Despite the fact that it's more road miles to go back the way we came, it will be less time spent in your car (and you kinda' know the way, right?).

The 20 Road is rocky and slow going past Wrangle Gap, but a good option if you have a capable vehicle and you seek the scenic route. For everyone who's in for the full tour, it's a short drive to our next turn-off. After leaving the PCT trailhead we'll drive southeast on the 2025 Road. As we continue down the road keep an eye to the right (south) as Donomore Meadow comes into view far below us.

At this point we're officially in the state of California and all the water that falls here as either snow or rain flows into California's section of the Klamath River.

The first intersection we arrive at is the road we want to the left (east), the 40S01 Road.

**Special Note:** Nearby Donomore Meadows are worth a visit.

To drive to the meadows, stay on the 2025 Road heading due south from the 40S01 intersection. There may be a sign near the intersection indicating Donomore Meadows are two miles ahead, but according to my odometer it's almost exactly one mile from the 40S01 intersection to the turn-off to the meadows.

After driving a mile, look for the second road (heads downhill) to the right; stay left at the "Y." The road can get rutted and muddy in wet weather as it goes downhill through some trees. The PCT edges along the southwest side of the grassy expanse and crosses Donomore Creek on a wooden footbridge before heading uphill and passing by an old herder's cabin on a knoll above the meadows.

The road to the old herder's cabin is steep with some clearance issues so best suited to four-wheel or all-wheel vehicles. There's potential for camping among the big trees on another rise south of the cabin. The fields can be green and awash with wild flowers in the early season; look for deer grazing on the greenery (along with the occasional free-range cow), listen for owls calling at night.

Constructed decades ago and now resurrected, years of heavy snows had nearly crushed the original structure. Open to the public and a popular overnighter for hikers on the PCT, the herder's cabin is in California just south of the Oregon state line. Please Respect It!

# 40S01 Road Intersection:

## 40S01 Road to Jackson Gap

The 40S01 heads uphill and northeast after leaving the 2025 Road. The road is not technically difficult so just about any vehicle (beyond a passenger car) with reasonable clearance can make it (with some probably tense moments). There's a potential campsite near the beginning, taking advantage of one of the few flat spots in this mountainous terrain.

The road is narrow and crosses a couple of minor washes as we gain elevation and cross the line back into Oregon. Big views of Mount Shasta begin to open up as we traverse the south side of Observation Peak. Although traffic is sparse it's possible to meet oncoming vehicles; make note of turn-outs. After reaching the high point, the 40S01 Road meets the 41S15 Road at a major intersection where we stay left on the 40S01 Road. The road from the intersection heads west and through the trees to its crossing below the eastern face of Observation Peak. If the weather is clear, park here and soak up the scenery.

## Cow Creek Glade Botanical Area

Several springs above and below the road form the headwaters of Cow Creek and the green, generally treeless meadow stretching below is called Cow Creek Glade. Mount Ashland is visible to the east, marked by the tiny-looking white radar dome atop its summit.

Looking west at the ridge marking the twin-peaked Observation Peak, you'll notice an old jeep road (that is closed to motorized traffic) heading steeply uphill. It's an easy hike to the south ridge line of the mountain following the old road, the steepest section being the initial climb to a three-way intersection. Keep right, following the road uphill to its end (elevation 7,140 feet) and a great view of Mount Shasta and your car below.

A sea of mountains surrounds you 360 degrees; soak up the high Siskiyou vibe. Looking north we're staring right at the Dutchman Peak Lookout cabin. To the south, the mountains of California's crest country are visible; the usually snow-capped Trinity Alps stand out that way. Heading back down the trail, look for a way to the right (west) and downhill to a curious old mine site.

*...oking east from atop Observation Peak we see Cow Creek Glade Botanical Area. Several ...all springs keep the area watered providing habitat for a variety of interesting plants. Mount ...hland is the high point left of center in the distance. The Road 40S01 meanders below.*

## Continuing north on the 40S01 Road

We gain some elevation as we leave the Cow Creek Glade behind and quickly arrive at **Observation Gap** and a **crossing of the Pacific Crest Trail**, elevation 7,022 feet.

The PCT basically parallels the road from here to its next crossing at Wrangle Gap.

From the PCT crossing, the 40S01 road heads due north as views open up to the southwest of Dutchman Peak and the beautiful meadowlands below us to the west.

Our next road intersection comes up quickly as we arrive at **Jackson Gap.** Map R1.2

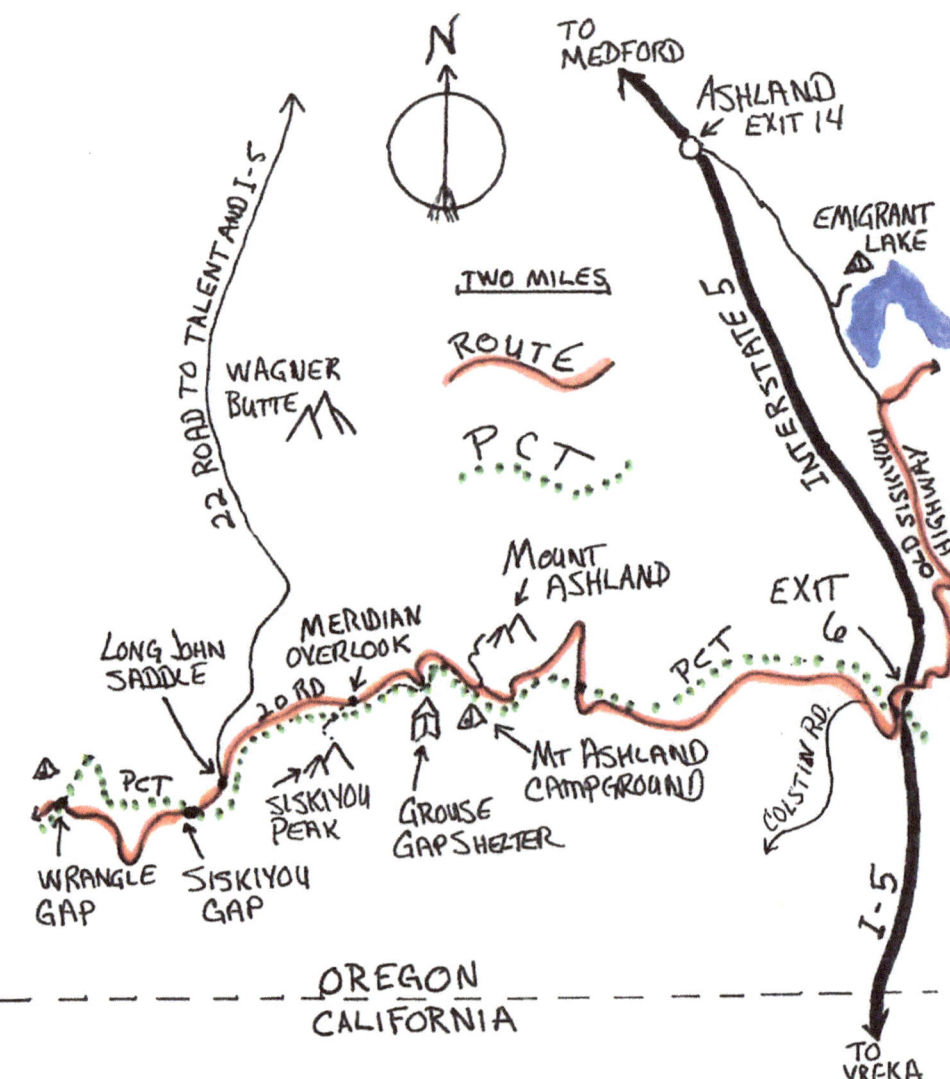

**Map R1.3: Wrangle Gap to Ashland and Emigrant Lake**

The 20 Road is rocky and slow-going from Wrangle Gap to Meridian Overlook. The stretch between Long John Saddle and Meridian Overlook gains about 1,000 feet in two gnarly miles and is not recommended for passenger cars.

It's an easy hike to Siskiyou Peak from Meridian Overlook. The road to the summit of Mount Ashland is worth the time if the weather's good. Take it slow and enjoy the big views.

*A Twisting Journey*

## Jackson Gap to Mount Ashland

**Note:** From Jackson Gap, we'll head east on the 20 Road to the paved parking lot for the Mount Ashland Ski Area. The 20 Road past Wrangle Gap is not recommended for passenger cars.

### Jackson Gap Area  *Elevation 7,028 feet.* **Map R1.2**

Usually windswept, Jackson Gap is a major crossroads along the Siskiyou Crest. At over 7,000 feet elevation, the plants and animals that maintain a toehold on this land are adapted to very harsh conditions; remember that at these elevations, the ground may be snow-free as few as 90 days per year.

Summer can be dry for weeks at a time and at first glance the porous ground can appear barren during the late season. Poke around a bit and you can discover several ground hugging and drought resistant plants not only thriving but putting on a showy wildflower display after the snows are gone.

This is a four-way intersection including the road we came in on. If the weather is good, now's your chance to visit the **look-out on the summit of Dutchman Peak,** elevation 7,434 feet.

The 800 Road is slightly offset from the intersection and the only road heading uphill from here; it's about a two mile climb (four-wheel drive recommended) to the look-out if the gate isn't closed. If the gate is locked and you choose to take the short hike to the look-out, park well below the gate to give other vehicles a place to turn around.

Manned during the fire season, the look-out offers a 360-degree view; the gate is usually closed around 7pm and re-opens around 8am to give the volunteer living at the station some privacy.

The 20 Road heading west from Jackson Gap will take you back to Silver Fork Gap. To continue our explorations, the 20 Road bearing east towards Mount Ashland is the one we want.

After leaving Jackson Gap, the 20 Road heading east follows near the true crest of the Siskiyous. The track finds its way through rock fields and big trees as the PCT follows us just below the road grade.

The 20 Road heads sharply downhill before arriving at the intersection marking Wrangle Gap.

## Wrangle Gap  *Elevation 6,505 feet. Map R1.3*

From Wrangle Gap we'll continue east on the 20 Road. It's about 3.5 miles to Long John Saddle. The PCT crosses the 20 Road near Wrangle Gap and skirts north around unimaginatively named Big Red Mountain. The road to our right (south) is the 40S12 road and angles its way downhill to a maze of unmarked logging roads. The 2030 Road heads north from the gap and in short order delivers the driver to Wrangle Camp.

The large, open-air building with a big stone fireplace is somewhat abused but undoubtedly excellent shelter from the storm for hikers on the nearby PCT. The structure bears the marks of a CCC construction and is listed on the National Historic Places register. The camp is situated below the crest on the north side of the divide protecting it from the wind.

The 2030 Road past the camp deteriorates quickly becoming steep, narrow, and brushy; I don't recommend further road exploration past the camp.

*Skyrocket gilia sets the hillsides ablaze in the High Siskiyous. The wildflower show begins in early June and lasts through the summer months on the high ridges.*

## Back on the 20 Road

The 20 Road past Wrangle Gap is wide and nicely graveled at first, luring the Sunday driver to continue. Things start to deteriorate as the track winds its way south around the flanks of Big Red Mountain, so don't expect to make time in any vehicle along this stretch of rough road.

Take it easy and pick your way through the rocky washes and (mostly) short uphill/downhill sections. Cheer up though, this is the worst part of the whole road (almost).

Look for places along the way to pull off and calm your jangled nerves. Grab the folding chairs and the binoculars and look for high altitude adapted species that inhabit the local woods.

This is a good place to spot mountain bluebirds and brightly colored lazuli bunting. Use your eyes and ears to spot soaring birds at eye-level. The roadway continues rocky and rough to our next intersection at Siskiyou Gap.

### Siskiyou Gap  *Elevation 5,866 feet*

> **Note:** From Siskiyou Gap we'll continue east on the 20 Road for only 1/2 mile (of rough road) before encountering Long John Saddle.

Another day, another gap. Long John Saddle is just ahead.

### Long John Saddle  *Elevation 5,857 feet*

> **Note:** This intersection is a tangle of roads with inadequate signage so if you haven't been here before (and even if you have) stop and get oriented before continuing.

Look around in the trees for signs and at the road options, the 20 Road east to Grouse Gap and Mount Ashland is the way we want to go.

Not a gap but a saddle you say? This low-spot is wider (and more saddle-like) than the other "gaps" perhaps explaining the designation.

There are two secondary roads heading south leading to a maze of logging roads etched into the south slope of the Siskiyou Range.

The 2040 Road to the north is brushy and steep (like most roads on the north slope of the range) and hooks up with the Little Applegate drainage; not worth your trouble unless you live down there.

Immediately after leaving the Long John intersection we encounter the broad, well graveled 22 Road to our left. Heading downhill, the 22 Road invites us to go north to the town of Talent and Interstate 5.

This is your last chance to bail on the 20 Road and get back to 21st century America before the last 2.5 miles of rough road to Meridian Overlook and better roads.

Everyone in for the tour, the road heads uphill from here as we edge our way along the north side of the Siskiyou Crest.

## Long John Saddle to Meridian Overlook

OK this stretch of the 20 Road is what gives it a bad name, we need to gain about a thousand feet in elevation in the next two miles and things get ugly quickly as we depart Long John and head east.

There are actually remnants of pavement along this road but don't expect anything resembling highway conditions. The way is rough and slow going in any vehicle as we make our way steadily uphill through the rocks and ruts.

The good news is it's only about 2.5 miles from LJ to Meridian Overlook and much better roads. Look for views to the northeast for glimpses of Mount McLoughlin, a volcano astride Oregon's Cascade Crest.

*Early summer brings wildflowers and cloudy weather in the High Siskiyous; perfect hiking conditions in other words. Siskiyou Peak is an easy hike from Meridian Overlook and a good place for your dog to look for those pesky squirrels.*

## Meridian Overlook  *Elevation 6,909 feet*

Looking at Meridian Overlook today is a bit of a head-scratcher. The metal sign adjacent to the parking lot lets us know that this is indeed, Meridian Overlook. There are a couple of stone works cemented together shaped in shallow arcs with no explanation.

Many years ago this was a developed site along the 20 Road and the pedestals had signs not only marking this spot where the Willamette Meridian crosses the road but information on the myriad plants and animals of the high Siskiyous. Today the place looks more like a Druid ceremonial center and for those of a ceremonial bent this is certainly a good place to perform a ceremony (of your choosing).

Or...hike the (illegal) tire tracks heading uphill from here and follow the high ground to where the PCT crosses below the south face of Siskiyou Peak.

The walk to the summit of **Siskiyou Peak** is easy but the high elevation will likely have you huffing and puffing before you get there. Trend to the left as you approach the pile of rocks making up the top. Look for stone cairns and follow the trail through the rocks to the peak, elevation 7,149 feet.

Your efforts will reward you with a sweeping view of the mountains to our south and west including a look-back view of Cow Creek Glade, the Trinity Alps, and California's Mount Shasta. I highly recommend the hike if you have the time and energy; better yet, throw some water and a sandwich into your knapsack and have a picnic on top.

## Meridian Overlook to Grouse Gap Intersection

The 20 Road improves steadily as we proceed towards Mount Ashland Ski Area. A few blocks past Meridian Overlook the tread passes just above the PCT as both the trail and the road swing north. It's at this point (where the road tops out near 7,000 feet elevation) that a snowdrift sometimes accumulates and blocks the road until July (in heavy snow years).

The big views to the south begin to open up and the mountainsides can be awash in wildflowers early in the summer season; look for glowing fields of red skyrockets, royal purple larkspurs, and creamy yellow stonecrop among the ancient rocks. The way zigs and then zags before losing some altitude and arriving at the Grouse Gap intersection.

*It's a party at Grouse Gap Shelter. Smoke rises from the chimney as this family enjoys a cook-out. The structure, open on two sides, is a popular destination from the Mount Ashland Ski Area, used by cross country skiers in the winter and day-hikers in the warmer months.*

**Grouse Gap Area** *Elevation 6,606 feet at the road intersection*

Typically there's a car or two parked here in the hiking season, this wide spot in the road is a popular trailhead for day-hikers on the Pacific Crest Trail. The PCT parallels the 20 Road and crosses a secondary road below it. The secondary road forks left before delivering drivers to **Grouse Gap Shelter**. The shelter, built of timber and stones, is open on two sides and comes complete with a large stone fireplace.

During the snow season the shelter is a popular destination for Nordic skiers and snowshoers coming from Mount Ashland. There's often a fire glowing to warm your frosty fingers.

The summer and early fall can serve up some beautiful weather and the long days of July and August can bring blue skies and glowing colors before the leaves fall.

The springs (above the shelter) at Grouse Gap provide for lush vegetation so take the time to explore compact Grouse Gap Glade for a sampling of high country flora.

## Grouse Gap to Mount Ashland Summit Road

After leaving Grouse Gap, the 20 Road continues its winding way eastward, contouring the southern flanks of Mount Ashland. Before reaching Mount Ashland Campground, we'll encounter a road angling left and heading uphill; this is the road to the top of Mount Ashland.

## Mount Ashland Summit Road

Not recommended for passenger cars (not sayin' you can't make it in the '99 Ford Taurus, just sayin' I'm not recommending it...).

The secondary road is rather steep and mildly rutted in places so probably not suited to low riding passenger cars. For those with more capable vehicles, take the 1.5 mile drive to the parking lot atop the mountain and soak up the amazing views.

The actual summit rocks (marked by the cemented bolts that supported the now gone fire lookout) are a short walk from the parking area. Mount Ashland, elevation 7,533 feet, is the tallest peak in the Siskiyou Range and from the top the views stretch to the horizon in 360 degrees.

The giant "eyeball" near the summit houses a Doppler radar. The 28 foot diameter radome shelters the rotating radar dish originally installed in 1996 and more recently upgraded with new technology to better predict severe weather in the region.

Leaving the Mount Ashland Summit Road, we'll continue east on the 20 Road towards Mount Ashland Campground. The PCT follows the road just below the grade.

## Mount Ashland Campground  *Elevation 6,670 feet*

So perhaps you'd like to spend the night here on the rooftop of Oregon? Now's your chance! One of the most spectacular campsites in the state, the views looking southward at glacier-carved Mount Shasta are magnificent on a clear day.

The campground is laid out on both sides of the 20 Road with most of the campsites above the road. The camp has 8 sites, picnic tables, fire rings, and vault toilets, but no water. Some sites are walk-in only. There are informational signs regarding the unique plants and animals found on the surrounding mountainsides.

Grab your binoculars and gaze at the tiny-looking trucks on I-5 (many miles away) as they pull the grade to Siskiyou Summit, the highest point on Interstate 5. At night around the campfire (bring your own wood) look at the incredible star filled skies.

Yes, all of this and it's free, available on a first-come first-served basis. June and July are the best months for wildflowers and butterflies. August and September are probably the best months for camping when the weather is more consistent and the skeeters are done.

After leaving the campground behind, we'll drive just 0.3 miles to the end of the 20 Road and the paved parking lot for the Mount Ashland Ski Area.

*Gazing south from the Mount Ashland Summit Road, California's Colestin Valley is centered in this photo. Mount Shasta is seen partly shrouded in smoke from wildfires burning in California. The views from the top of Mount Ashland stretch out in 360 degrees. The distinctive nipple of Pilot Rock is visible to the left.*

# Mount Ashland to Emigrant Lake and Highway 66

## Mount Ashland Ski Area
*Elevation 6,630 feet where the asphalt begins (or ends)*

The 20 Road becomes County Road 1151 at the ski area. Our next turn is 9 miles ahead at the stop sign and Highway 99.

After driving miles and miles of beautiful backroads along the Siskiyou Crest we are unceremoniously delivered to a paved parking lot, part of the Mount Ashland Ski Area. The 20 Road is gated at this point when the snow flies.

The acres of asphalt marks the end of Forest Road 20 and the beginning of Jackson County Road 1151 (a.k.a. the Mount Ashland Ski Road).

Drive on through the parking lot like you own it and just around the bend you'll find more asphalted parking acres next to the buildings and lift infrastructure of the Mount Ashland Ski Resort operation.

This is the only commercial ski area in Southern Oregon. Covering a few hundred acres and served by five chair-lifts, the sometimes fickle snows have challenged the resort in recent years, pushing them near the financial edge. Perhaps turning the corner after a series of drought years, a string of more recent winter storms has left the summit of the mountain stacked with more than 10 feet of snow during the first week of spring. Because of the relatively high elevations, an average of 300 inches of snow in a twelve month period can be expected to fall on Mount Ashland and the Siskiyou Crest.

Big snow makes happy skiers and that translates to not only money in the bank for the resort but ample run-off to local streams and lakes. Stay tuned ski fans... After leaving the ski area, the Mount Ashland Road heads down the mountain in a series of switch-backs; the PCT follows closely.

Two miles down the road we'll encounter a formal trailhead and parking lot for the PCT, elevation 5,987 feet. The road continues downhill providing more awe inspiring views of Mount Shasta to the south and the distinctive form of Pilot Rock to the east.

The road-cuts have exposed the interesting and complex geology of Mount Ashland; look for turn-outs where beautiful scenery and interesting rocks are on display.

About 7 miles from the Mount Ashland Ski Area we come to the intersection with the Colestin Road.

## Colestin Road Intersection

How interesting can a boring old road intersection be? I'll leave it up to you to answer that (deep) question, but there are several stories that converge here.

The oldest story is that of the local rocks. Jackson County, Oregon road crews have a chore maintaining the road at this juncture because it keeps slipping away. One can almost guarantee that there will be safety cones and other markers warning drivers of the dangers here.

Why are things so fluid at this particular spot? The answer lies in the geography here. The local mountains (the "Klamath Knot") consist of collections of rocks of different age and composition moved here via the conveyor belt of plate tectonic forces. The distinct collection of rocks that make up Mount Ashland are called a "pluton."

Now mind you, I know just enough about the subject of Geology to embarrass myself around someone who actually does understand it, but as I get it, a pluton is a "hot-spot" bubble, an intrusive body of liquid rock that is crystallized as it slowly cools, particularly interesting to miners.

You may have noticed the light colored rocks along the road-cut as you descended the Mount Ashland Road, these are characteristic of the eastern edge of the "Mount Ashland pluton." Now look east at the "fin" of rocks making up the eastern edge of the Colestin Road Intersection and you can see where the light colored rocks abruptly meet the much darker rocks of the "fin," angling upwards from the slow-motion collision with Mount Ashland. It's at this junction or fault that the Colestin Road heads south.

This crossroads marks where these different rock masses are sutured together. These two formations don't dance to the same rhythm though, causing sheering forces between them and guaranteeing Jackson County road crews headaches for decades to come.

*A look-back at the Mount Ashland Ski Area from the Colestin Road intersection shows the Giant Eye Ball and the many ski runs served by the area's five chair lifts.*

*Past the traffic cones stands the Clamper's monument. The Colestin Road marks the intersection of human and geological history. And guaranteed work for Jackson County road crews.*

*The interesting and complex geological history of the Siskiyou Mountains is on display at the Colestin intersection. These rocks have stood witness to thousands of years of human travel across these mountains.*

The human story begins with the First People of North America who lived for thousands of years in the valleys to the north and south of the Siskiyou Crest. There is ample evidence that groups of people traveled through, lived and hunted in this vicinity (during the warmer months) and used this low-point crossing to travel between the Klamath and Rogue River Valleys.

Look to the north side of the Colestin Road Intersection and you'll see a three-sided monument donated in 2016 by the **Southern Oregon "Clampers"** (I googled "E Clampus Vitas") of the Umpqua Joe Chapter 1859 based in Cave Junction, commemorating the modern history of this place (Thanks Clampers!).

The famous explore**r Peter Skeine Ogden** was employed by the Hudson's Bay Company to trap beavers for their pelts and document the rivers and mountains of the Pacific Northwest. Guided by local Native Americans, Ogden and his group of trail-hardened trappers crossed this low-gap pass on February 9th, 1827.

A second group of Hudson's Bay Company trappers crossed here in 1829. Led by Alexander McLeod, it was this group that named the pass "Siskiyou" after a native word for bob-tailed horse.

A foot path for millenia, the pass had developed into a major wagon road by about 1850. An influx of miners from California crossed the Siskiyous en masse after word got out of the gold strike near Jacksonville in 1851; many of the "51ers" crossed the Siskiyous here.

Escalating tensions between settlers and natives and an attack on supply wagons by native people in 1855 near this spot led to the Rogue River Wars (1855–56) and the forced removal of the surviving First People to far away reservations.

A regular stagecoach route across the pass began in 1860 and was part of the "Great Road" connecting Sacramento, California with Portland in the newly minted state of Oregon. The stage route operated until 1887 with daily departures running north and south. The stations to the north and south of the steep road topping the Siskiyous were key in the operation of the wagon road. We'll learn about Oregon's **Barron's Station** as we pass-by on our way down Old Highway 99.

Turn onto Colestin Road and follow its winding way south down the old stage road about 8 miles to the California town of Hilt and the still standing **Cole's Statio**n which saw the last wagon roll by in late 1887, coinciding with the opening of the rail tunnel beneath Siskiyou Pass.

Cole's Station was the southern anchor of the old wagon road across the Siskiyous. Usually an overnight stop, fresh teams of six horses were harnessed-up for the pull across the Siskiyou Pass and the next stop at Barron's Station in Oregon. Today it's a private residence.

The last wagon pulled out of Cole's Station in late 1887. The just completed rail tunnel under the Siskiyou Pass signaled its demise.

After the American Civil War, the U.S. began building railroads and rail companies eyed Siskiyou Pass as the logical place to dig a tunnel to cross the mountains. Dug by Chinese workmen laboring from both ends, Tunnel 13 was completed in 1887 and lies below your feet as you stand at the Clamper's monument.

This was **not only the final link for rail travel between California and Washington State to the north, but its opening also completed rail lines around the circumference of the United States.**

Just looking at the above stories you might say this is an interesting place indeed. But wait, we're not done yet…Tunnel 13 was the site of a famous Oregon train robbery featuring the bungling **DeAutremont brothers.**

In 1923 the three brothers hatched a plan to rob the train as it chugged the last slow yards up to the pass. Two of them commandeered the locomotive and forced the engineer to position the mail car just outside of the tunnel. The other brother, using an overly generous charge of dynamite, blew the mail car to smithereens (I've always wanted to use that word) killing the clerk.

An ensuing gunfight killed three more railroad employees as the empty-handed brothers made good their escape, evading a massive manhunt by hiding under a downed tree for days. The brothers split-up from the scene of the crime and avoided capture until 1927 when they were sentenced to prison.

Portions of the old wagon road in Oregon were incorporated into Highway 99. Before there was such a thing as Interstate 5, Highway 99 was the main drag along the west coast and is still known as the Pacific Highway.

The local portion of I-5 was constructed in the 1960s and crosses the Siskiyous just to the east of the Colestin Road Intersection at Siskiyou Summit (not Siskiyou Pass), where the old Wagon Road, Highway 99, Interstate 5, and the PCT all come together.

Who would have thought that so much was going on at this boring little, nondescript hunk of dirt?

## Old Highway 99 Intersection
*Elevation 4,258 feet at the intersection*

**Note:** We'll turn left (north) at this intersection and drive to the stop sign at Exit 6.

Our route heads north from the stop sign and in short order **crosses the PCT**. There's a small parking area for the trailhead here. The trail heads south and crosses below I-5 nearby.

Just more than 1/2 mile from the Mount Ashland Road brings us to another stop sign and the I-5 interchange at Exit 6.

Turn right (east) at the stop sign and pass under I-5 following the signs to Old Highway 99 and Highway 66.

*Callahan's Lodge has expansive landscaped grounds and a huge deck overlooking it all. The lodge is hiker friendly and offers package deals for hikers on the PCT. The interior of the lodge is comfortable and cozy with a welcoming fire on chilly days. The nineteen luxury rooms feature a fireplace in each. Live music is heard on most weekends.*

# I-5 Interchange at Exit 6
*Elevation 4,041 feet*

It's about 8 miles to Ashland via the evil I-5 but fortunately for us, there's another way down the north slope of the Siskiyou Mountains that doesn't involve playing chicken with behemoth trucks and in-a-hurry motorists. After crossing beneath the freeway and heading east on Highway 99 (also called the Old Siskiyou Highway) we'll see the entrance to Callahan's Lodge.

## Callahan's Lodge
541-482-1299

Originally built by World War II veteran Don Callahan on a site about a mile north of the present operation and subsequently demolished for the construction of Interstate 5, the lodge was reconstructed on this spot in 1965. Sold in 1996 and expanded by owners Ron and Donna Berquist, the lodge was leveled by fire in 2006.

Reborn from the ashes is today's Callahan's Lodge with fine dining, banquet facilities, and nineteen luxury rooms with fireplaces in each. Now owned by Mark and Lisa Cleaner, the lodge has 23 rooms, a four bedroom house and a campground.

For hikers on the PCT, the lodge offers storage of re-supply parcels, and package deals that include a hot shower, laundry, a bottomless plate of spaghetti, breakfast, camping, and a free beer for $80. Tent camping for PCT hikers is currently $30 per night (2023 prices). A corner of the huge, nicely landscaped backyard presently serves tent campers. There's a deck overlooking the grounds and live music can be heard on most weekends.

## Old Highway 99 to Highway 66

The Old Siskiyou Highway heads downhill from Callahan's in a series of switchbacks, following the old wagon road for the most part. Big trees grow next to the road and it can be icy in the winter but even when the weather's warm and the roadway is bare, it's slow going. Take your time and enjoy the ride as the road passes over itself like a snake eating its tail.

The railroad also chose this way down the mountain and after passing through the tunnel dug beneath the Siskiyou Summit, the track nearly doubles back on itself in a couple of very long switchbacks.

*Rich in Southern Oregon history, this restored structure is the oldest documented wooden building in the area. Founded in 1852 by three partners shortly after gold was discovered near Jacksonville, it became **Barron's Station**, the first stop in Oregon for northbound travelers on the California to Oregon stage line.*

## Barron's Station

Before reaching the junction with Highway 66, keep an eye to the left for 1148 Old Highway 99 and you'll see the large yellow farmhouse marking this historic building. There's a plaque in the front yard noting that this was once an important stage stop called **Barron's Station.**

Rich with history, this is the oldest (documented) wooden structure in Southern Oregon. Founded by three partners in 1852, the traveler's inn and tavern was built at the crossroads of the **Siskiyou Pass Trail** and the pioneer road called the **Applegate Trail.** Fortunately for the partners, gold was discovered in Jacksonville about the same time the inn was being completed and business was good from the get-go.

A wagon road was eventually constructed crossing the Siskiyou Mountains and in 1860 the California Stage Company began providing daily service from Sacramento to Portland Oregon.

The station was named after the surviving member of the original partnership, Hugh Barron. Mister Barron was a very busy man who married and had three children. While the family ran the inn, Mr. Barron farmed and ranched the broad valley raising vegetables, cattle, horses, hogs, and sheep.

Even after the contract with the stage companies ended in 1887, the businesses thrived as a flood of emigrants descended on Oregon in the ensuing years. The Barron family eventually controlled nearly 8,000 acres of land.

Changing hands in 1960, the land holdings were pared down and the buildings were allowed to deteriorate to the point of junk-filled ruins by the time the property was again sold in 2002. The new owners spent more than two years lovingly restoring the station and converting it to one of the premier B & B's in Southern Oregon, operating for almost ten years. The property changed hands once again in 2014 and is currently a private residence.

### Emigrant Lake and Highway 66 Intersection

Driving past Barron's Station, we quickly arrive at the stop sign and the intersection with Oregon Highway 66. While this intersection marks the end of Region One and the beginning of our Region Two explorations, we'll take the time to visit nearby Emigrant Lake Park and the city of Ashland before continuing.

Turning left (north) at the stop sign, it's less than a mile to the turn-off to Emigrant Lake County Park (described in Region Two). The city of Ashland lies about 3 miles northwest from the park entrance.

> **Note:** Wanna' skip the city of Ashland and follow the PCT? Turn right at the stop sign and follow Highway 66 to Greensprings Summit. See the Region Two Route Description on page 71.

## End of Region One

*A serene summer morning reflects in the calm waters of the small lake near the eastern entrance to Ashland's leafy Lithia Park. Perfect for a leisurely stroll, the park stretches for more than a mile following Ashland Creek uphill.*

# Region Two
## City of Ashland to the town of Fort Klamath

*Downtown Ashland is centered on what locals call the "Plaza." Surrounded by several blocks of interesting shops and restaurants, this is the gateway to Lithia Park and Ashland Creek.*

"Started out for
God knows where.
Guess I'll know,
When I get there."
~ **Tom Petty**
*Learning to Fly*

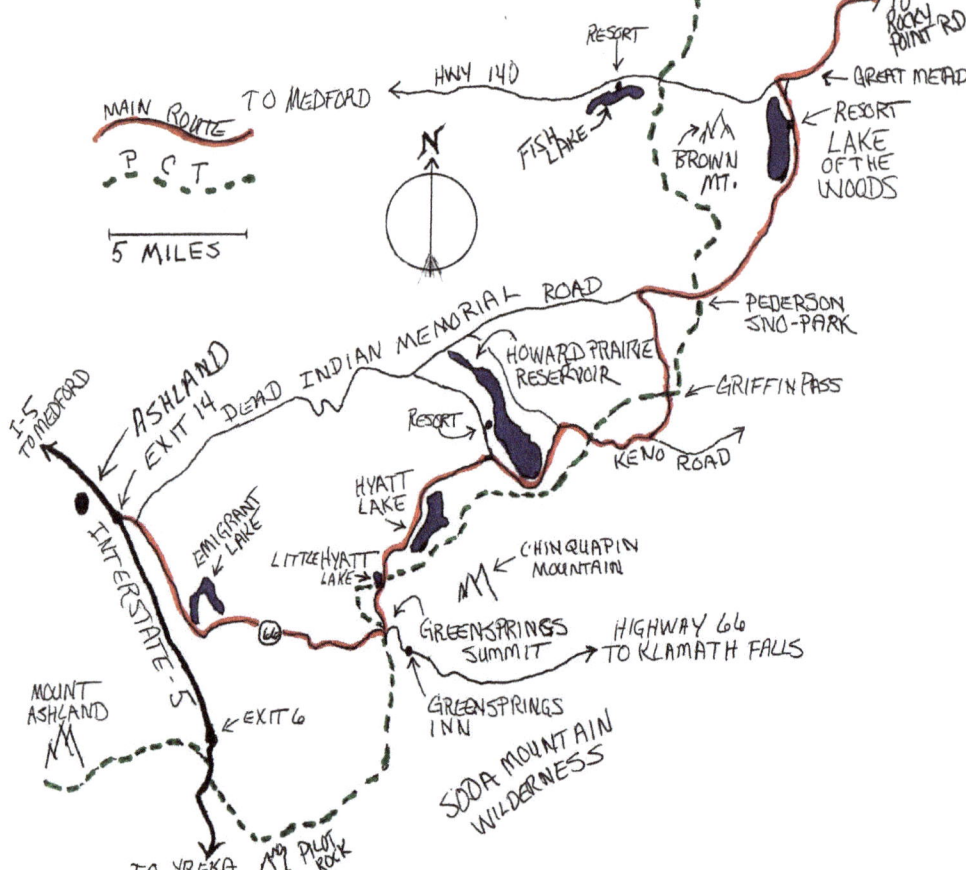

## Map R2.1 City of Ashland to Highway 140

*Map R2.1 shows the road route paralleling the PCT from Green Springs Summit to Oregon Highway 140. This half of Region Two has many interesting lakes, large and small, to visit. With five lakes, four resorts, several campgrounds, and plenty of fishing and hiking opportunities. It's easy to spend a day exploring this area. The Region Two description continues past Lake of the Woods to the tiny town of Fort Klamath.*

# REGION TWO MAIN ROADS IN ORDER OF TRAVEL

## Beginning in Ashland:

### Highway 66
Green Springs Summit and Little Hyatt Road intersection.

### Little Hyatt Road
Gravel road past Little Hyatt Lake to Hyatt Prairie Road.

### Hyatt Prairie Road
Paved road…It's a short drive north to Howard Prairie Dam Road.

### Howard Prairie Dam Road
A dam fine paved road. Hooks up with Keno Access Road.

### Keno Access Road
Access to Keno was important, I guess? Paved, takes us to Forest Road 2520.

### Forest Road 2520
Improved gravel road to Griffin Pass. May also be designated as Big Draw Road on Google maps, delivers us to…

### Dead Indian Memorial Road
Not sure about the name but I think it's meant in a positive way? Paved road to Lake of the Woods Resort Road intersection.

### Lake of the Woods Resort Road
Our connection to Highway 140.

### Highway 140
State Highway connection to Rocky Point Road.

### Rocky Point Road
Paved road turns into improved gravel.

### West Side Road
Paved highway past Rocky Point takes us to the 3100 Road.

### Forest Road 3100
Dirt road takes us past beautiful riparian areas.

### Nicholson Road
Paved road to the town of Fort Klamath and the end of Region Two.

# Optional Roads and other Attractions Described in Region Two:

**Fish Lake Resort:**
Hiker friendly near where the PCT crosses Highway 140.

**Buckhorn Road:**
Gravel Road Option to Highway 66. This is the route followed by the Applegate Wagon Trail.

**Howard Prairie Recreation Area:**
A resort, cafe, gas, camping, RV hookups, extensive marina and fishing jetty.

**Green Springs Inn and Restaurant:**
Great food and luxury cabins, outdoor dining, popular with cyclist. Less than 2 miles east of Green Springs Summit.

## PCT ACCESS POINTS IN REGION TWO

From Ashland the two nearest places to get hikin' on the PCT are Highway 66 at Green Springs Summit, trail mile 1,733, and the I-5 crossing, south of Ashland near exit 6, trail mile 1,716.3. **Map R2.1**

Many section hikers start at I-5 and hike NOBO (northbound) to Crater Lake or head south (SOBO) across the Siskiyous to California.

Besides those two places the most significant trail crossings for day hikers and section hikers in Region Two are at Pederson Sno-Park on the Dead Indian Memorial Road, trail mile 1,759, and the crossing at Highway 140 between Fish Lake and Lake of the Woods, trail mile 1,770.9. **Map R2.1**

> **Special Note:** Although the City of Ashland isn't officially on the PCT, we begin this route description at I-5, Exit 14 mostly to keep things simple. Besides, Ashland is such an important part of most Southern Oregon travelers' experiences we would be remiss in not including it in these descriptions.

# REGION TWO ROUTE DESCRIPTION:

The road route begins at Interstate-5, Exit 14 in Ashland, travels past five major lakes, and ends at the town of Fort Klamath, Oregon. This route is mostly paved with short stretches of improved gravel, suitable for any vehicle. There are no clearance or traction issues in good weather and snow-free roads. Total distance is around 90 miles. Allow (with some stops) from four hours to a couple of days. Ashland is the last reliable place for fuel.

From I-5 Exit 14, Oregon Highway 66 heads east to the crest of the Cascades. Turning north from Highway 66 at Green Springs Summit, our route follows the PCT and the Cascade Mountains past Little Hyatt, Hyatt, and Howard Prairie Lakes.

After crossing 5,730 foot Griffin Pass we drive northeast past Lake of the Woods and Upper Klamath Lake. Region Two ends at the tiny town of Fort Klamath where there are no services.

Because of the rolling nature of the Southern Oregon Cascades, elevations can be deceiving. Griffin Pass, elevation 5,730 feet, is an un-plowed road in the winter and among the higher road passes in the Oregon Cascades. This pass and the approach roads leading to it are typically closed because of snow during the winter and into the late spring and sometimes until early summer.

Other State Highways and most paved county roads along this route are regularly plowed during the winter but may close during heavy snow events. Remember to take the season into account when planning a trip to the high country and go prepared with chains and a shovel during winter months.

## MAPS FOR REGION TWO

For paper map geeks I recommend the Rogue River National Forest Visitors Map and *Benchmark Maps-Oregon Road and Recreation Atlas* pages 85, 96, and 97.

The Rogue River Forest Map overlaps the Winema National Forest roads that are part of Region Two. Updated versions may be available soon. order U.S. Forest Service maps online at **fs.usda.gov/rogue-siskiyou**. The Cascade-Siskiyou National Monument and the Soda Mountain Wilderness area are administered by the Bureau of Land Management (BLM).

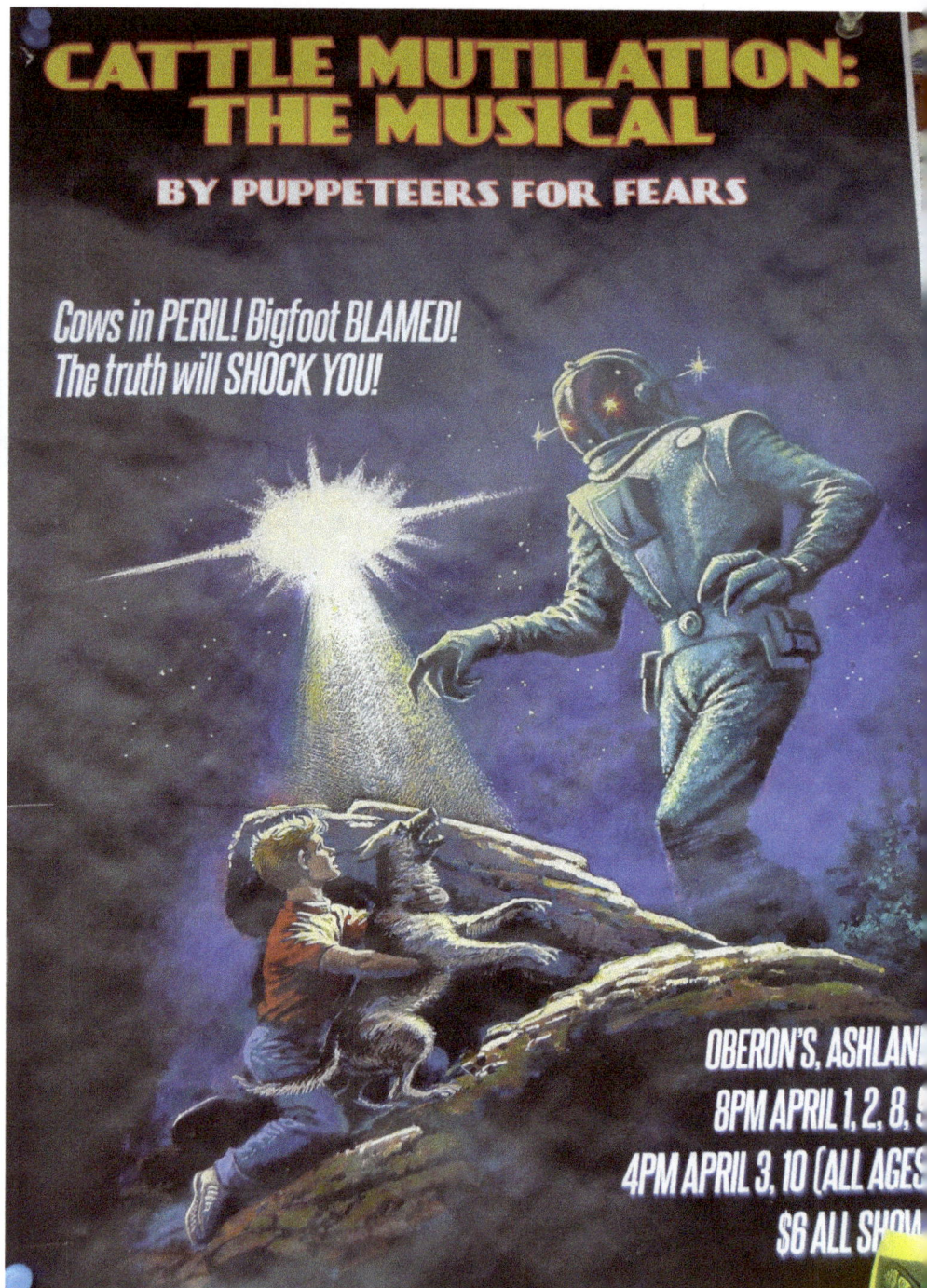

Ashland is well known for its theater scene and the creative humor of local actors and writers. I found this poster advertising a riveting drama in the Ashland Plaza. The truth will shock you!

# ROAD NOTES FOR REGION TWO

**Ashland**  *Elevation 1,990 feet at Exit 14*

This route begins in Ashland at the intersection of Siskiyou Blvd and I-5 exit 14, the south Ashland exit. We head southeast on Oregon Highway 66 from there.

Ashland has my vote as the best Oregon town along the I-5 corridor. Sure, Eugene has the award for funky weirdness (to my friends in Eugene, I mean that in the best of ways), and Portland gets the prize for big city soul and bohemian ambiance, but Ashland's happy mix of laid-back hippy cool and artistic sophistication makes it the hands-down winner. Maybe there's something in the water (actually there is something in the Lithia water) but the mostly friendly natives and beautiful surroundings (nestled between the Siskiyou and Cascade Mountains), and a generally sunny climate, it's really not even a close contest.

The city is one of the main attractions to hikers on the Pacific Crest Trail. Few towns of any size are located near the trail in Oregon. Many section hikers choose to either start or end their hike near Ashland while thru-hikers (those whose goal is to hike the entire 2,650 mile trail from Mexico to Canada in one season) often choose to rest and re-supply here.

Wander around the side streets and discover trendy restaurants and other flavorful businesses. With a cozy bar and a friendly crew **Louie's Bar and Gril**l, located downtown on the Plaza, offers good food and an impressive menu of reasonably priced dishes. Try Louie's version of meat on a stick, "Flame Grilled Skewers," served with a spicy peanut sauce.

Take time to explore **Bloomsbury Books**. Established in 1980, this independent bookstore and coffee shop checks all the boxes. With an outdoor garden, it's easy to spend a couple of hours browsing the ecclectic collection of books here. They also feature local authors.

The **Oregon Shakespeare Festival** is an important player in the Ashland scene (yes, puns fully intended), as are several other theaters that stage live performances in Ashland and surrounding communities throughout the year. Get more info online at **osfashland.org**.

### Is there something in the water?

*Well... yes there is. The massive cast iron fountain in the Plaza serves up water from Lithia Creek. Lithia Creek is located east of downtown and not associated with Ashland Creek that flows through Lithia Park. I noticed that there weren't a lot of takers for the free repast. Locals enjoy inviting visitors to sample the bitter tasting mineral water.*

## Lithia Park

With the Tudor Style buildings of the Oregon Shakespeare Theater looming above the entrance, the park follows Ashland Creek uphill and stretches many acres to the west of town (about 1.4 miles) enticing the stroller with trails, duck ponds, and an ice skating rink in the winter.

The park is linear in nature with informative plaques (including the many signs reminding everyone Not! to feed the ducks) describing the history of the park along with botanical and common names of the diverse plantings of trees and shrubs inhabiting the riparian area of the creek. Interspersed with the playground equipment are eclectic garden sculptures. Volleyball and tennis courts are present for the athletically inclined.

In the company of our (sometimes odd) fellow men and women, the park offers many opportunities to linger and enjoy the sound of falling water and experience nature in a near natural environment. Trails connecting uphill from the park lead to the Ashland Watershed and a connection with the Pacific Crest Trail.

## Ashland to Green Springs Summit

From Exit 14 in south Ashland we head east on Oregon Highway 66. It's 14.8 miles to Green Springs Summit and the turnoff to Little Hyatt Road.

At 0.5 miles from town we pass the intersection of Dead Indian Memorial Road on our left. We'll encounter this road later in our journey. Still heading east on Highway 66, we encounter Emigrant Lake Park Road 3.1 miles from exit 14.

## Emigrant Lake Park  *Elevation 2,241 feet*

> **Note. Attention Geology Nerds!** Just before the entrance kiosk, rounding the curve to our left, is an interesting example of what's known as the **Hornbrook Formation.** A late Cretaceous marine deposit, this unassuming band of fist sized and smaller cobblestones and fossilized sea shells embedded in the road-cut were formed when this was ocean front property. No gently sloping sandy beach here, the cobbles are evidence of a wave-tossed shoreline.

The park consists of two separate camp areas; one for RVs (32 sites) and the other for car and tent campers (42 sites). Large day-use shelters can be rented for group events. Food concessions and showers are available near the 280 foot waterslide which is operated seasonally. While not a heart stopper, the slide is good wet fun on a hot day.

Emigrant Lake is open for fishing year 'round with at least one of the area's two boat launches open in the winter. The fish in the lake run the gamut from several warm water species to trout. Check your local regulations before fishing.

Leaving Emigrant Lake Park we continue east on Highway 66 and intersect Old Highway 99 (the end of Region One) 5.0 miles from exit 14, elevation 2,285 feet. Continuing a few miles east on Highway 66 the road grade is mostly flat, watch out for cyclists.

At 7.7 miles from exit 14, we encounter the Optional Buckhorn Road on our right.

> **Special Note:** For those who choose not to take the Optional Buckhorn Road, The Main Route (marked in red on the Guide map) continues below at: **Still heading east on Highway 66.**

## Optional Buckhorn Road
*This optional road is marked in yellow on the Guide* Map R2.2

Buckhorn and Tyler Creek Roads are improved gravel, OK for passenger cars. This optional road heads in the same direction as Highway 66 but stays at lower elevations before climbing steeply and re-joining Highway 66 just west of Green Springs Summit.

There are other roads leading off this one that get you closer to trail heads that lead into the Soda Mountain Wilderness and connections to the PCT. This was part of the historical route of the wagon road called the Applegate Trail and winds past ranch and farm operations as it makes its way towards the Cascade Crest.

Madrone stands mixed with pine and conifers line the creek drainage. Watch for wild turkeys along the way. This road heads southeast along Emigrant Creek before heading east along Tyler Creek Road.

Two miles from Highway 66 we come to a Y in the road. Tyler Creek Road is to our left, heads uphill, and leads us back to Highway 66. The road to our right leads to a gated turn-around and the entrance to Buckhorn Springs Retreat.

## Buckhorn Springs Retreat Center
*2200 Buckhorn Springs Road 541-488-2200*

The Center features several cabins for rent and the chance to experience the potential healing properties of the local $CO_2$ springs. These springs are reputed to be the sacred springs of the Native Americans who inhabited this area for thousands of years, with stories of on-site medicine men who administered the proper "prescriptions" of vapors for the gravely ill.

Warring tribes declared a temporary truce for those who could reach the springs. Legend tells us that those who led virtuous lives in the eyes of the Great Spirit would be healed, while those that were lacking would face a less rosy future. Learn more about this enigmatic place at **buckhornsprings.org**.

# Tyler Creek Intersection
*From the Tyler Creek Intersection it's four miles to Highway 66.*

We ascend the valley through beautiful open woodlands towards the rocky outcrop of Hobart Bluff. 2.5 miles from the Tyler Creek Intersection we arrive at Baldy Creek Road (40-3e-5.0). Keeping to the left we continue uphill.

As we near Highway 66 the views get better, Pilot Rock is in clear view to the southwest. Turn right on Highway 66 (uphill) and arrive at Green Springs Summit in less than 0.5 mile. (See Green Springs Summit Intersection described below).

*Take me home, country road. The Optional Buckhorn Road offers up some beautiful fall scenery. Look for deer and wild turkeys amid the rural backdrop.*

# Still heading east on Highway 66
*For those not taking the Optional Buckhorn Springs Road.*

Highway 66 is narrow in places with few opportunities to pull off as we leave the Buckhorn Road behind and head uphill. The scenery gets better as we come to a pair of small turnouts on the right, 12.0 miles from I-5 Exit 14, elevation 3,651 feet.

Stop and admire the southern view of Pilot Rock, elevation 5,909 feet, the core of an old volcano. Pilot Rock has been an iconic landmark for travelers through this region for thousands of years, marking one of the low spot east/west routes through the Southern Cascades along with the north/south way through the Siskiyous.

On the uphill side of the Highway 66 road-cut, check out the layered, twisted rock exposed here and further uphill, evidence of the titanic forces that shaped these mountains.

Looking east from here we can see the Cascade Crest approaching on the horizon and 14.8 miles from Ashland we intersect the Soda Mountain Road on our right as we arrive at Green Springs Summit and the trailhead for the PCT.

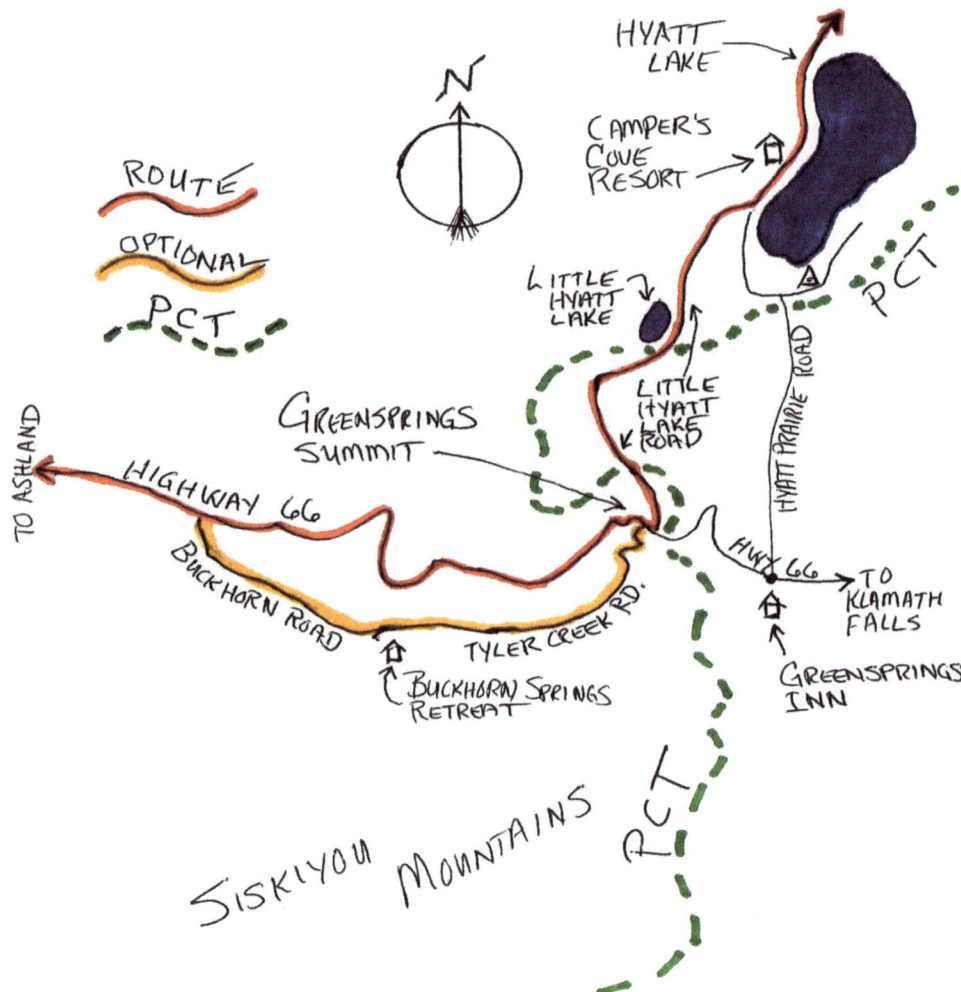

**Map R2.2: Green Springs Summit Area**

*Map R2.2 shows the optional Buckhorn Road. Green Springs Summit is an important crossing of the PCT. The road route turns off Highway 66 at the summit and follows Little Hyatt Lake Road north to Hyatt Lake. Green Springs Inn is a short drive east from the summit on Highway 66.*

A Twisting Journey

## Green Springs Summit Intersection  *Elevation 4,570 feet*

The PCT crosses here. We'll leave Highway 66 and follow the improved gravel Little Hyatt Road as it heads north from the Green Springs intersection following the PCT.

> **Important Note:** Green Springs Inn and Restaurant is less than two miles east of the summit on Highway 66 (towards Klamath Falls) and is well worth a visit for the hungry and/or weary traveler. So before we leave Highway 66 and drive north on Little Hyatt Road let me say a few words about the nearby Green Springs Inn and adjacent Cascade Siskiyou National Monument.

*Early Summer and sunshine greets visitors to the Green Springs Inn. Cyclists with iron lungs and calves of steel pedal the Highway 66 grade from Ashland. The lodge serves as the informal center of the Green Springs community.*

## The Green Springs Inn and Restaurant  *Elevation 4,534 feet*
541-890-6435

The Cascade-Siskiyou National Monument Information Center is located next to the restaurant.

There's more to the Green Springs Inn than meets the eye. Typical winter conditions at this altitude can mean plenty of snow, bringing bright days when the sun shines.

Early summer sun translates into blue skies and an explosion of wildflowers in the surrounding hills and meadows. The restaurant features great steaks, homemade soups and breads, and delicious salads and desserts. They also serve a hearty breakfast and lunch with juicy burgers and fries.

Good food and friendly service seems to be their goal. There's a small selection of camper items in the store and a nice selection of beers on tap and in the cooler. Live music on the weekends and a summer mountain music festival add to the smile-on-your-face feel of the Green Springs Inn.

The country surrounding the Inn is ground zero for the Cascade-Siskiyou National Monument. The proximity of the Soda Mountain Wilderness combined with the many other recreational opportunities in the area puts the Inn at the center of many new four season activities. The Inn also offers a free beer to all thru-hikers on the PCT.

A surprising number of people (considering the elevation) live year-round in the immediate area and the Inn serves as the hub of the Green Springs community; functioning as the meeting place for local news, good food, conversation and toe tappin' live music.

The Inn is situated on 150 acres and also rents nine beautiful, privately located cabins overlooking Keene Creek. Each stoutly constructed (there is a sawmill and a solar heated lumber kiln on the property) and nicely appointed structure features a hot tub or custom tiled shower. Along with luxurious cabins, the Inn offers lodging in an eight room motel. Mountain bikers can find lots of opportunity to ride nearby. Cross country skiers and snowmobilers can headquarter here in the winter.

## The Cascade-Siskiyou National Monument

This land is unique in that it was chosen as **the first National Monument in the Northwest to preserve biological diversity** rather than designated for its scenic or geological attractions.

A convergence of biological influences from the Cascades, Klamath/Siskiyou Mountains, and Great Basin habitats have shaped the local plants and animals here. Largely spared the heavy glaciations of the last Ice Age (which ended more than 11,000 years ago), this crossroads of Northern California, Southern Oregon, and the Great Basin hosts an amazing diversity of life. The Soda Mountain Wilderness is contained within the National Monument and lies just south of the Green Springs Inn.

## Little Hyatt Road

This improved gravel road heads north from Green Springs Summit and crosses the Pacific Crest Trail in 1.1 miles. We pass a few incongruous mini-mansions along this road before encountering Little Hyatt Lake, 2.7 miles from Green Springs Summit.

*The PCT crosses Keene Creek on a wooden footbridge just below the Little Hyatt Lake spillway. Springtime brings blue skies and flowery meadows to the Cascade high country.*

### Little Hyatt Lake  *Elevation 4,645 feet, no facilities*

A small dam forms this lake. The PCT crosses a footbridge along the south side of the lake and the short hike over the dam to the west side of Little Hyatt offers unimproved campsites for walk-ins on BLM land. On the road past the dam, there's a small turn-out to the left; a good place to throw a stick for the dog, go swimming, or just relax and watch the fish ringing the surface.

Leaving Little Hyatt Lake we continue north on Little Hyatt Road. Stay right at the fork, it's less than 1.5 miles to the pavement.

## Hyatt Lake Intersection  *Elevation 5,031 feet*

At the stop sign, Hyatt Lake lies before us. Turn left to go to Campers Cove Resort and the continuation of our road route, or right to explore **nearby Hyatt Lake Campground** and the east side of the lake (both described below).

To the south and east of Hyatt Lake stands **Chinquapin Mountain**, elevation 6,134 feet. Its namesake, the chinquapin tree (or "giant" chinquapin) is a northwest native and related to the chestnut. This hardwood tree is evergreen with attractive shiny leaves and generally occurs on the north side of slopes. Its spiny coated seed pods with tiny edible nuts (not worth the trouble) help identify this hardy tree.

*The attractive leaves of Chinquapin shine in the winter sun. This Pacific Northwest native is one of few broad leaf evergreens in the high country. Tough conditions makes tough wood. Early European settlers to the Willamette Valley were short on metal tools for farming and used the fire-hardened wood of the chinquapin to shape rudimentary plows.*

## Hyatt Lake Campground and the East Side of Hyatt Lake
*Elevation 5,020 feet at the boat launch*

For those purists and Google map readers, there appears to be a road that goes through on the east side of Hyatt Lake (East Hyatt Lake Road) that more closely follows the PCT. This road has been gated for years and perhaps the mapmakers will catch-up soon.

From the campground entrance it's a short walk east to a connection with the PCT. There's a nice BLM campground on the east side called (oddly enough) **Hyatt Lake Campground**. The sprawling campground features 2 boat ramps, 47 pull-through camps and 7 walk-in sites.

Camping in the park is reservation only but the day-use area is first come first served with a self-pay station at the entrance. Contact **recreation.gov** for more information.

Fishing for perch can be good family fun with still-fishing seemingly the most popular method. Try a piece of worm 3 feet under a bobber. Children of all ages can look for some fun playground equipment adjacent to the day-use area.

Just past Hyatt Lake Campground, **Wildcat Campground** is smaller and located on a peninsula. The road ends at a gate shortly after the entrance to Wildcat Camp. There's a pleasant campsite for PCT hikers in the woods to the east.

Because the East Hyatt Lake Road is gated, there are some places to park along this quiet side of the lake that give you the opportunity to walk through some relatively undisturbed high country wetlands and meadows. This can also be a good place to cross country ski/snowshoe in the wintertime. Look for osprey nests, diving cormorants, and other plants and animals of the marshes and mountain woodlands.

## Camper's Cove Resort
*7900 Hyatt Prairie Road, 541-482-3331*

The resort has a café (with an extensive menu and pretty darn good food) and a small store. Cabins are for rent year-round. During the summer season kayak and canoe rentals are available.

Camping, fishing, bird watching, and boating are the pastimes here in the summer time. Snowmobiling and cross country skiing are popular in the winter months.

Fishing for (mostly small) bass in the lake can be productive. Some occasional lunker bass weighing over 5 lbs. are hooked here. Every year a few rainbow trout are caught measuring well over 20 inches, big enough to eat the many smaller bass.

Continuing less than 0.5 miles north on Hyatt Lake Prairie Road, we come to the Osprey Viewing Area with a lakeside bench and informational signs describing the typical birds that may be seen from here. From the viewing area it's 3.8 miles to Howard Prairie Dam Road.

See the next page for the "**Howard Prairie Dam Road Intersection**" description and the continuation of the Main Route.

> **Special Note:** Howard Prairie Recreation Area and the adjacent Howard Prairie Resort and Marina lies 1.5 miles north of the Howard Prairie Dam Road intersection along the Hyatt Prairie Road. Below is a description of this nearby attraction.

## Howard Prairie Lake Recreation Area  *Elevation 4,526 feet at the lake*

For information on camping at Howard Prairie Lake Recreation Area take a look at the excellent website **jacksoncountyor.org**

Howard Prairie Lake Resort operates a small store along with a café and marina. A rock jetty extends into the lake providing shelter for the marina and handicap accessible fishing.

The resort rents deluxe RV trailers with hookups, boats, kayaks and canoes. RV, tent and car camping are available in the adjacent campground. Gasoline is available here for cars and boats.

**American White Pelicans** with wingspans generally over 100 inches are easy to spot; these birds are somewhat lumbering and not uncommon on Howard Prairie Lake and other area lakes. Sand Hill Cranes are sometimes seen in the marshes and open woodlands at this elevation. Often heard before seen, the three-foot tall adults are sometimes distracted and easy to find if approached slowly during the mating season (April and May) and are further identified by their red crests.

## Howard Prairie Dam Road Intersection   *Elevation 4,625 feet*

The continuation of the Main Route turns right and heads northeast on Howard Prairie Dam Road. From this intersection it's 3.8 miles to Keno Access Road.

Just 0.6 miles after leaving the Dam Road intersection we find Willow Point on our left. **Willow Point Campground**, located at the south end of the lake, features a popular boat ramp and a hiking trail (about 0.3 miles) to the **Red Rocks**, a good place for walk-in bank fishing.

2.5 miles past Willow Point we encounter Klum Landing on our left. **Klum Landing Campground**, located on the east side of the lake has a boat launch, camping, day-use area and showers. Leaving Klum Landing, keep an eye to your left for an unmarked dirt road. This road goes to an informal view point and rocky beach adjacent to the dam, a nice spot for a picnic or to let the dog go swimming. There's a small (no fee) slide-in boat launch here for canoes and smaller boats but no camping.

Back on the main road there's a dip as the road passes over the irrigation canal. Before we reach Keno Access Road, there are a couple of dirt tracks that head west towards the lake and a few informal campsites on the shoreline. Still heading northeast on the Dam Road (it's really not that bad!) we soon arrive at the **Keno Access Road Intersection**.

> **Note:** Anyone who writes a good travel guide has obviously spent a great deal of time exploring the areas they describe. Discovering secret places is part of the job description…so, with some trepidation (since I once hauled a pick-up load of trash out of there, and besides that there's always some "different" folks who like to camp-out in the woods), I share with my readers the **Secret Swimming Hole at the Old Quarry.** Please note that clothing is optional.

**Instead of turning right (the Main Route) on the Keno Access Road, turn left and head west.** I'll leave it up to you to discover exactly where the quarry is (about 3.7 miles) but look for layered rocks along the roadside adjacent to an unmarked road to your left. A pretty choice swimmin' hole if you don't mind someone looking at yours. Shhh! Don't tell anyone…Please pick up your trash.

*Clothing is optional at the (not so) secret swimming hole. During the warmer months the Quarry Hole is usually inhabited by a few, shall we say, uninhibited campers who insist on letting the software hang. All cool if you're good with that, right?*

## Keno Access Road Intersection
*Elevation 4.622 feet*

> **Special Note!** Our next turn-off is a possibly unmarked road. Check your odometer and **drive exactly 2.4 miles east** on the Keno Access Road to the Griffin Pass Road. **Do not turn on the 38-4E-34 Road!** Consult **Map R2.1**.

Heading east on the Keno Access Road it's a total of 2.4 miles from the Dam Road to our turn-off at the 2520/Big Draw Road to Griffin Pass.

Leaving the Dam Road behind we encounter a crossing of the PCT in 0.9 miles and past that we see the 38-4E-34 Road on our left.

Past that we come to a probably unmarked road to our left shown as **Big Draw Road on Google Maps,** a total of 2.4 miles from the Dam Road Intersection.

Although this road may or may not be signed, it's the Griffin Pass Road, also designated as the 2520 / Big Draw Road.

## 2520 / Big Draw Road Intersection  *Elevation 4,998 feet*

Leaving the Keno Access Road we'll turn left and head north across **Griffin Pass**. It's a total of 5.3 miles from this intersection to our next turn-off at Dead Indian Memorial Road.

There are remnants of pavement for the first mile of this road before turning to improved gravel. The road heads steeply up through scattered woodlands with some washboards but is suitable for any vehicle. Continuing 1.7 miles from Keno Access Road we reach Griffin Pass and the **intersection of the Pacific Crest Trail.**

*Jeffrey Pine* (pinus jeffreyi) *is named after its describer, botanist John Jeffrey. Jeffery worked as a gardener at the Royal Botanic Garden in Edinburgh, Scotland before traveling to Hudson's Bay in 1850 where he proceeded to travel overland to the Columbia River. Living and working in Washington, Oregon and California, Mr. Jeffrey disappeared while crossing the southern California desert in 1854 and perished at the tender age of 28.*

*Also known as yellow pine, the Jeff can grow to be more than 150 feet tall. Found mostly in California along the eastern Sierra, it ranges into southwestern Oregon. Pine cones form in distinctive whorls and are almost purple when immature. The Jeffery specializes in growing in nutrient poor soils unable to sustain most other tree species.*

### Griffin Pass Area  *Elevation 5,730 feet at the pass*

This pass (among the higher road passes in the Oregon Cascades) divides BLM land to the south from National Forest land to the north The drier southern slope is open grassland with scattered second and third growth timber. Big trees on the north side of the pass, marked by a cattle guard, delineate the National Forest boundary.

From Griffin Pass the PCT makes a sharp bend east as it skirts nearby **Old Baldy Peak** before starting to head north in earnest. The Pacific Crest Trail follows the crest of the Cascades making its way through the expansive Sky Lakes Wilderness before delivering hikers to Oregon's only National Park, Crater Lake.

**Big Spring** (about 150 yards south of the Griffin Pass summit) provides an easy near-trail water supply when it's producing for PCT hikers passing through here. Flowing from a pipe, the cold, clear water (not tested for drinking quality) is a refreshing treat on a hot day. Near to the spring is a single walk-in campsite suitable for PCT hikers, tucked into the trees.

The National Forest side of the pass (north) has some nice stands of more mature trees with some good areas for a rambling walk. The surrounding area is a prime place in the fall to hunt for chanterelles and other edible mushrooms. Heading north from Griffin Pass we drive through beautiful stands of big firs and pines, crossing Big Draw Creek as we head downhill (watch out for the dips in the road) and meet up with Dead Indian Memorial Road.

### Dead Indian Memorial Road Intersection  *Elevation 4,814 feet*

We'll turn right and head east on Dead Indian Memorial Road from this intersection. It's 11.2 miles to our next turn-off at Lake of the Woods Resort Road 3750.

3.4 miles from the Griffin Pass Road we encounter the **Pederson Sno-Park**, elevation 5,380 feet and the **intersection of the Pacific Crest Trail**. It's here we cross over into Klamath County and enter the Winema National Forest.

Before our turn at Lake of the Woods Road, we encounter a housing development (what?) of large rusty-roofed homes, and a major intersection where we'll continue straight (east) on the DIM Road. Keep an eye out for our turn north on the Lake of the Woods Road.

**Lake of the Woods Resort Road 3750** It's a short drive to the resort's driveway so keep a sharp eye to the left. From the resort entrance to the intersection of Highway 140, it's one mile.

## Brown Mountain  *Elevation 7,340 feet*

This is the dominant geographical feature as we head northeast from Griffin Pass towards Lake of the Woods. Brown Mountain is a serious volcano in its own right. While not as impressive visually as its 9,495 feet counterpart to the north (Mount McLoughlin), Brown Mountain and associated vents have produced some impressive amounts of lava (as tall as a 25 story building in places).

The mountain is a cinder cone perched atop the larger shield volcano (as opposed to a steep-sided stratovolcano like Mount McLoughlin) overlying many square miles of volcanic activity. Looking in places like the magma just cooled off last week, the lava fields present a natural barrier to backpackers heading north along the Cascade Crest. The PCT crosses large sections of vulcan landscape as it heads north towards its rendezvous with Highway 140 and beyond to the Sky Lakes Wilderness.

Fortunately for us this eruption is older than it looks, occurring thousands of years ago, (the last eruptions appear to be well over 2,000 years old), and road builders have been busy working their way around it. An excellent place to view Brown Mountain is from the boat ramp at Lake of the Woods Resort.

*Early spring finds the near shore of Lake of the Woods ice-free. The view from the boat launch at the Resort includes the eastern side of Brown Mountain, a recently active volcano that has produced prodigious amounts of lava. The PCT passes through extensive fields of volcanic rock as it traverses the western side of the 7,340 foot volcano.*

## Lake of the Woods Area  *Elevation 4,960 feet at the lake*

For info on camping and to make reservations take a look online at **recreation.gov**.

Located in a deep chasm between lava cloaked Brown Mountain to the west and the 7,700 foot-plus peaks of the Mountain Lakes Wilderness to the east, Lake of the Woods covers 1,146 surface acres and supports a healthy fishery. It's also one of the most popular places to recreate in Southern Oregon.

Fisherpersons be warned, on hot summer weekends the water skiers and jet skis take over the lake in the afternoons.

Fishing for rainbow trout and kokanee is the main pastime here for fishermen (and fisherwomen too). Some impressive brown trout inhabit these waters and Lake of the Woods is one of the few lakes in Oregon open to night fishing.

Many cabins and year round residences dot the shoreline but since this is National Forest land, the entire shoreline is open to bank angling. Check local regulations before fishing. Camping is available at the resort and two other popular campgrounds on the lake.

## Sunset Campground

Located about midway along the east side of the almost four mile long lake, this is where the summer time action is. With 64 campsites, water and fire rings, this huge and heavily used campground/day-use area is within walking distance (about a mile) of the Resort and the Rainbow Bay picnic area.

There are no hookups but all sites offer RV parking. Sunset Campground also features a boat ramp and adjacent beach area.

## Aspen Point Campground

This extensive campground features a boat ramp and day-use area with a connection to hiking and mountain biking on the High Lakes Trail leading to Fish Lake. If there is such a thing as a low-key campground on the lake, Aspen Point is it.

Featuring 50 RV sites and a few walk-in tent sites closer to the lake; the resort is an easy walk from here.

## Lake of the Woods Resort  *Elevation 4,956 feet*

Established in 1922, the sprawling resort consists of the store and marina at the boat ramp and a separate bar & restaurant that were updated in 2011. With boat rentals and fishing licenses available at the marina, an outdoor BBQ and live music on a lakeside stage many summer weekends, Lake of the Woods is one of the top destination resorts in Southern Oregon.

The resort rents cabins with two nights minimum and has 25 RV sites. During the summer months the resort hosts an all-you-can eat barbeque and live music on their lake-front stage. There's room for dancing next to the stage and a bonfire is lit for after music relaxation.

The bar is cozy (and has the nicest bathrooms in the Southern Cascades) with a great selection of Oregon micro-brews on tap. The restaurant serves up hardy food and is open for breakfast, lunch and dinner during the summer. Auto gas is available at the store and boat fuel is available dock-side.

*A fisherman tries his luck at Lake of the Woods. The snowy presence of 9,495-foot-high Mount McLoughlin frames the horizon to the north of this natural lake.*

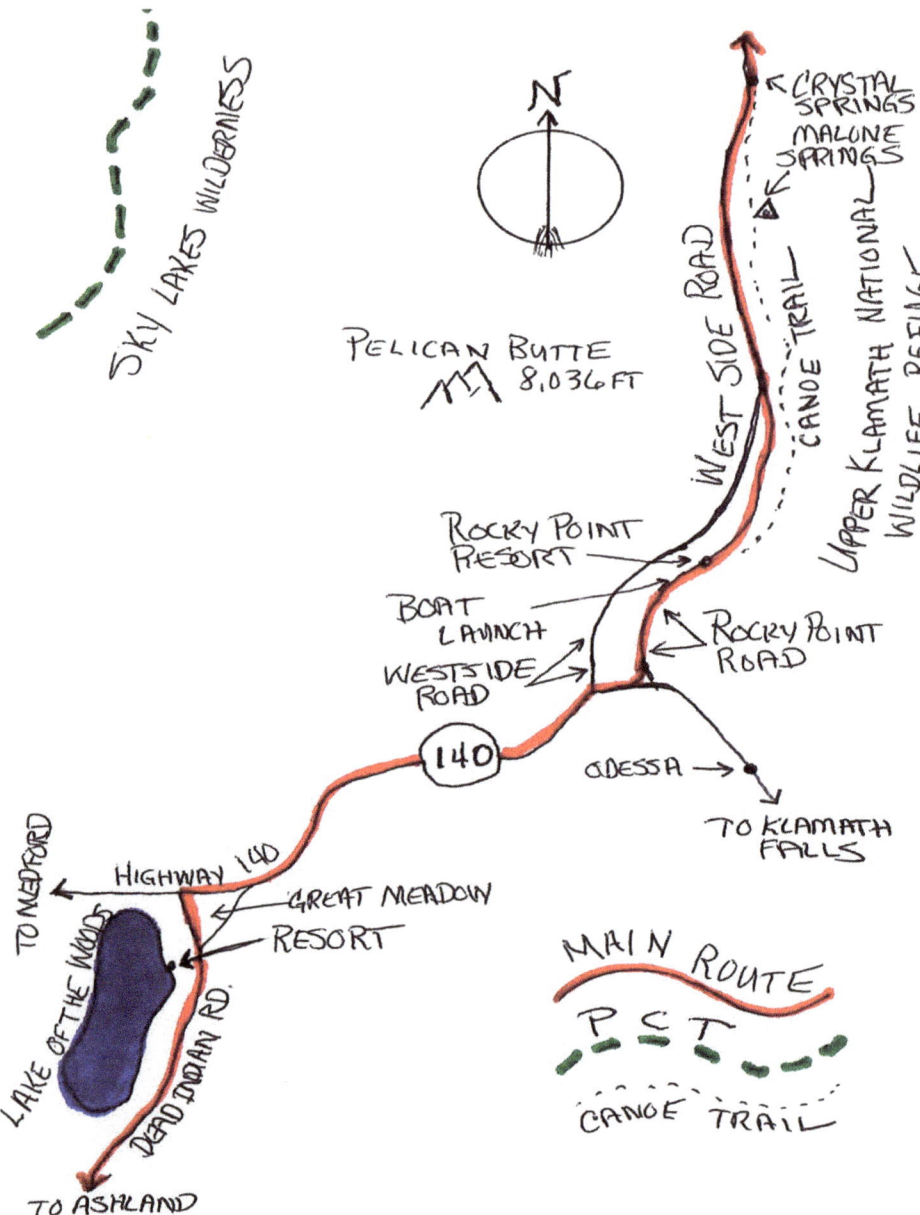

## Map R2.3  Lake of the Woods to Crystal Springs

*Lots of things to see and do at Lake of the Woods and nearby Upper Klamath Lake. The canoe trail through the National Wildlife Refuge begins near Rocky Point Resort and stretches to Crystal Springs. The canoe trail offers paddlers a gateway to fishing, bird watching, and serenity.*

## Highway 140

We head east on Highway 140, 7.2 miles to the Rocky Point Road turnoff. If you turn the other way (west) on 140 and drive a couple of miles you will arrive at the **PCT trailhead** adjacent to Highway 140, trail mile 1,770.9, elevation 4,970 feet.

Most hikers on the PCT head for the hiker friendly **Fish Lake Resort** for rest and resupply. Their number is 541-949-8500.

The resort has a small cafe, laundry and showers, and they accept resupply packages for $5.

**Important Note!** Before reaching the Rocky Point Road, we encounter the major intersection and turn-off to Crater Lake/Fort Klamath on our left (the Westside Road). Don't turn there, proceed another 0.4 miles east on Highway 140 to the signed **Rocky Point Road turnoff** and the continuation of the Main Route.

Fish Lake Resort has an extensive menu for hikers and hungry fishermen. There's a deck and several picnic tables scattered about the grounds. Hikers on the PCT can count on juicy burgers and fries and of course, ice cream! We tried the sweet potato fries, pretty dang good with ranch dressing...

## Lake of the Woods to Rocky Point Road  Map R2.3

From Lake of the Woods Resort Road we turn right on Highway 140 and head east past the **Great Meadow**. Features like the Great Meadow are somewhat common in the Southern Cascades but few are as big as the Great Meadow. Scooped out originally by ice fields, shallow lakes were formed when the climate warmed.

Sediment has helped to filled them in. In the case of the Great Meadow, drainage ditches were dug in the early twentieth century to help the process along (for better or worse). There's a large parking area to accommodate the snow park, restrooms, and an information board.

Before Highway 140 turns sharply north, we pass the intersection marking the eastern end of Dead Indian Memorial Road on our right.

Looming directly above of us as Highway 140 heads north is **Pelican Butte**, elevation 8,036 feet. From our perspective this shield volcano looks uniform but the northeast side (much like Mount McLoughlin) has been scooped away by glaciers. The bowl is easily seen from Fort Klamath and is popular with snowmobilers and backcountry skiers.

A ski resort was once proposed for this mountain, money swapped hands, some regulators passed judgment but nothing has yet happened. Pelican Butte lies well east of the Cascade Crest and despite its (impressive for this neck of the woods) elevation, rarely gets enough regular snow to support a commercial operation. There's a lookout on top with a 360-degree view, are your eyes good enough to spot it from Highway 140?

In 6.8 miles from Lake of the Woods Road we arrive at the intersection of the Westside Road with a sign indicating Crater Lake and Fort Klamath to our left. **Don't turn here**, this is the county high-speed road and has surprisingly little exposure to Upper Klamath Lake.

To get a better look at the lake and the town of Rocky Point, the Main Route continues east on Highway 140 another 0.4 miles to the **signed turn-off to Rocky Point Road**. We'll meet up with the Westside Road again in 5.2 miles.

***Special Note!*** The tiny burg of Odessa lies about two miles further east on Highway 140 (towards Klamath Falls). There's a small store with gas. Nearby is a compact Winema Forest campground on Odessa Creek with a steep dirt boat launch. Odessa is the closest place to fuel-up (short of driving to the town of Klamath Falls), and for those following this guide through Region Three, the last place to fuel-up before the station at Diamond Lake.

## Rocky Point Road

We stay on this road for 5.2 miles to its junction with the Westside Road.

Turning north on Rocky Point Road we wind past many homes and cabins. This place gets its name from the fact that most of Klamath Lake shorelines are mucky and shallow, making landing a boat or building a structure difficult. Rocky Point rests on a solid shelf of basalt with a fairly deep and sheltered harbor. Before the roads were improved in the area, a regular ferry and mail boat ran from the town of Klamath Falls to Rocky Point and Odessa.

*Established in 1899, Harriman Springs Resort and Marina has first class facilities and was for sale as of 2020. The Lodge was newly constructed in 2014 and features an expansive deck. Aspen Butte, elevation 8,215 feet, in the distance.*

Heading north on Rocky Point Road, look for the sign for Harriman Springs. Beautiful **Harriman Springs Resort** and Marina were newly constructed and upgraded in 2014. The expansive grounds, modern lodge, and substantial marina is a haven for Klamath boaters from paddlers to power-boaters and sailors. As of this writing (2020) the entire operation was for sale. Hopefully the new owner will continue to operate this landmark as a resort open to the public. Stay Tuned!

The Point Comfort Lodge was constructed in 1912 and is listed as a National Historic Landmark. There are two very attractive cabins on the property with fully furnished kitchens.

On the lake side of the road, look for the *Point Comfort Lodge*, 831-475-7306 or on the web. Built in 1912 this structure and its furnishings represent the classic "grand" lakefront lodge of the period. The Lodge has 7 bedrooms and 5 baths and a huge fully equipped kitchen.

There are also two very attractive cabins for rent on the Point Comfort property, the Carriage House comes fully furnished, sleeps three comfortably and rents from $150 a night with two nights minimum. The more rustic 1940s Cabin also is fully furnished and sleeps four, $160 per with two nights minimum. Both cabins have furnished kitchens and provide bed linens.

## Rocky Point Boat Launch

2.5 miles from Highway 140 we arrive at the paved Rocky Point Boat Launch. This is the southern end of the **Upper Klamath Lake Canoe Trail** with adequate ramp and docks to accommodate much larger boats. The dock also provides wheelchair accessible fishing.

Launch your canoe here and paddle south about a half mile along the shore to the mouth of Harriman Creek. Head up the creek (with a paddle) past the Resort and gaze at the giant trout that are usually pooled there in the summer; while Klamath Lake is open to fishing year 'round, check the regulations before fishing the tributaries. At the head of the creek, **Harriman Springs** flows from the rocks.

## Rocky Point Resort

Located on an arm of Upper Klamath Lake connecting to Crystal Creek, the resort is owned by the Oregon Odd Fellows. Many serious (and sometimes odd) fishermen from around the Northwest converge on the lake during May and June in search of rainbow trout up to 15 pounds. No sir, that's not a misprint…15 pound (and no doubt larger) trout swim these waters.

A news item from several years ago recounts the story of a six foot-plus sturgeon hooked and fought in view of witnesses lining the Rocky Point Resort deck. It's not hard to accept these fish tales as true when you look at the thousands of acres of interconnecting lakes, marshes, springs and rivers making up the Upper Klamath Basin.

The restaurant serves dinner at lakeside with every table a view seat. Pot roast is a favorite among guests. A small store attaches to the office and offers beverages, snack items and fishing tackle.

The resort rents power boats along with canoes and kayaks during the April 1st through October 31st season. There's boat fuel at the marina.

Trailer sites with power and water are available during the summer and early fall.

Lodging is basic, the four cabins have a small kitchen and along with five motel rooms, a couple of campsites next to the lake are also available.

The Rocky Point Resort lodge rests upon a rocky point. Many serious fisher persons frequent the waters of Klamath Lake targeting the big trout grown in these environs. The resort lies near the southern end of the Klamath Canoe Trail.

*A campsite with a view. Looking south from Rocky Point we see Aspen Butte, a steep sided shield volcano. Upper Klamath Lake is the largest lake in Oregon. The lake and surrounding marsh lands are popular with bird watchers and fishermen. This campsite is available at Rocky Point Resort.*

## Upper Klamath Lake  *Elevation 4,143 feet*

This is the largest freshwater lake by area in Oregon and the largest freshwater lake west of the Great Lakes. Popular with bird watchers and fishermen, this wetland along with its connecting rivers grows some big trout (see above!). Look for American White Pelicans, Sand Hill Cranes, and American Avocets in these environs.

Once upon a time the Klamath Basin spanned over 180,000 acres of shallow lakes and marshes. Headwaters to the mighty Klamath River, these diverse wetlands attracted prodigious flocks of birds along with fish and amphibians. Native people have inhabited this area for thousands of years harvesting the rich bounty of this generous land.

Today the Klamath Basin is much changed. The Bureau of Reclamation began in 1905 to drain the wetlands and create agricultural and ranch land. Perhaps 25 percent of the originally extensive marshes and shallow lakes remain today. The U.S. Fish and Wildlife Service in cooperation with the Bureau of Reclamation run the show in the Klamath Basin.

These agencies have (un-enviably) tried to balance the needs of wildlife and the sometimes competing wants and needs of modern ranching and agriculture. The **Klamath Basin National Wildlife Refuge** is dedicated to protecting what's left.

The diverse wetlands and forests of the reserve still attract millions of migratory birds yearly. The Klamath Basin National Wildlife Refuge is divided into six individual refuges. The Upper Klamath Refuge extends along the northwest side of Upper Klamath Lake and includes the **Upper Klamath Canoe Trail.**

"You go first!" Rookie paddle boarders embark on their shaky maiden voyage at Malone Springs. The informal campground and small boat launch is a popular place to get on the Klamath Canoe Trail. Not much here except an informational sign and an outhouse. Bring the binoculars, bird watching can be very good in this marshy environment.

## Upper Klamath Canoe Trail

The canoe trail leads paddlers through some primal marshland. Bird watching is, of course, unavoidable, birdsong and wind through the rushes fills the air most days. Different routes head north to south. The boat launch at Rocky Point represents the southern end of the water trail and Crystal Springs anchors the northern end of the trail. Malone Springs Campground and boat launch are in the middle.

## 3525 Intersection with West Side Road

Here we'll turn right and head north on the Westside Road. It's 11 miles from here to our turn-off on the 3100 Road. In 0.8 miles we encounter the Malone Springs Road on our right.

## Malone Springs

Drive this short road towards the lake and find a small camp area with a boat launch suitable for launching canoes and kayaks. The campsite is unimproved with an outhouse facility. Malone Springs is a popular launch point for day paddles south to Rocky Point. Head north from Malone Springs and paddle to Crystalwood Lodge. Back on the West Side Road its 3.4 miles to Crystal Springs Recreation Site.

*The very dog friendly Crystalwood Lodge is adjacent to the Crystal Springs Recreation Site. The Lodge has acreage for you and your dog(s) to romp and play. The property has waterfront on Upper Klamath Lake with canoes and rowboats to paddle about.*

## Crystal Springs Recreation Site

Its 6.8 miles from here to our turn-off on Forest Service Road 3100. There are restrooms located here with handicap accessible vault toilets. Originally the site of a school, it's at the northern end of the Upper Klamath Canoe Trail now.

This is a popular place for birding and is part of the **Klamath Birding Trail**.

For more information on bird watching opportunities in the Klamath Basin and the Upper Klamath National Wildlife Refuge, look online at: klamathbirdingtrail.com.

Adjacent to the recreation site is Crystalwood Lodge.

## Crystalwood Lodge
*866-381-2322*

For those who choose to travel with a pack of dogs (three or more) you know the look you receive when you check in to any place of lodging, eyes wide open with a wary look.

If you're the proud master of oh…let's say five dogs, you probably need a guide book of your own for those places that will accept you and your pack. On that very short list of accepting places would be the Crystalwood Lodge.

Perched on the northern end of the canoe trail, the lodge is all about dogs. The owner has raced her dogs in the Iditarod and the seven rooms in the lodge are each named after a waypoint on the Alaskan sled dog trail.

Every cozy room has its own bath, dog crates, and wool mattress pad. Guests have communal access to a fully furnished commercial kitchen and outdoor grill. The common area is ample and the grounds are expansive with canoes and places for dogs to splash and play just down the hill.

Paddling and bird watching are popular activities. Bring your Wi-Fi capable devices if you must…the lodge provides connectivity.

## Heading north on the Westside Road

**Special Note!** After leaving Crystal Springs, the Westside Road takes the driver north for several miles before the road curves sharply east. It's at **this curve in the highway we meet the intersection of the 3100 Road.** If you find yourself driving east on the Sevenmile Road, you've gone too far. **Refer to Map R3.1**

## Forest Service Road 3100
*Your Google maps may show this as NF-33*

The gravel 3100 Road heads north along the rocky shelf edging the Upper Klamath Basin and is **suitable for any vehicle with caution**. It's basically an unpaved extension of the Westside Road.

Some maps show this by-way as the 3300 Road and some show it as the Westside Road, your smartphone might say **NF-33**. Regardless of designation it's a beautiful three mile drive along the western rim of the Upper Klamath Basin.

Numerous springs flow eastward just below the road bed. About a mile from the pavement the views to the east open up. Stop and look for the many springs large and small that line the hillside below the road. Just past the first springs look for bigger views across open meadows.

In 2.8 miles from the West Side Road we encounter an intersection where we stay right and head east on the 3100 Road.

In about 0.3 miles we leave the Winema National Forest and the 3100 Road becomes the paved Nicholson Road.

## Nicholson Road

The Nicholson Road transitions from trees to range land as it heads east through wide open spaces taking us in a straight shot to Jo's Motel and the **town of Fort Klamath.**

# End of Region Two

*A twisted gargoyle guards the rim above mysterious Wizard Island. Crater Lake is Oregon's only National Park and is open 365 days a year.*

# Region Three
## Town of Fort Klamath to Lemolo Lake

The official Pacific Crest Trail stays well below the rim of Crater Lake with not a peek of the lake itself. Most backpackers choose to hike a series of connecting footpaths along the western rim of the volcano with attendant crowds and distracted drivers part of the scenery.

> "You belong among the wildflowers
> You belong in a boat out at sea
> Sail away, kill off the hours
> You belong where you feel free"
> - **Tom Petty**
> *Wildflowers*

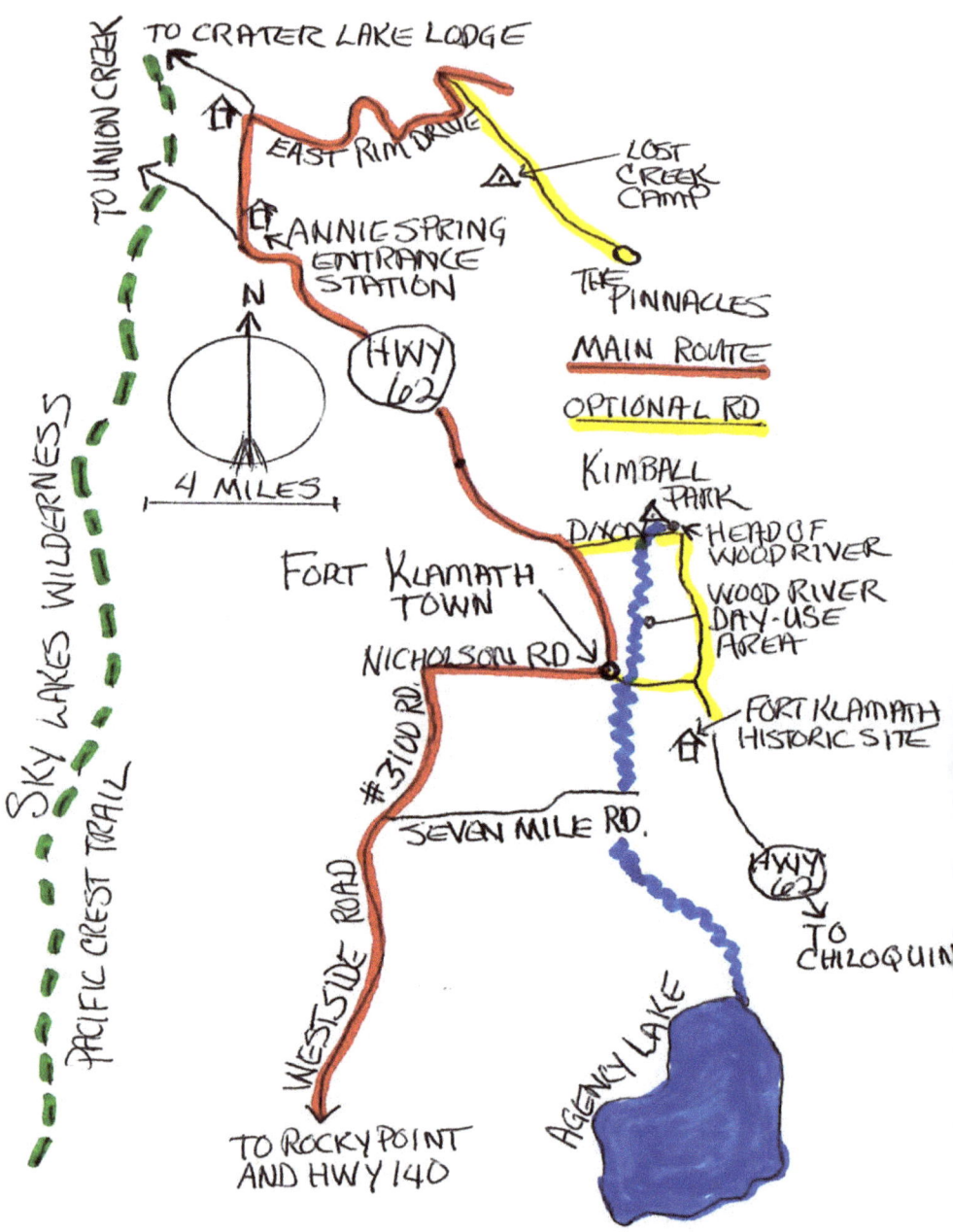

**Map R3.1 Town of Fort Klamath to Crater Lake**

The optional Wood River Loop is worth your while. Take a gander at the headwater springs of the Wood River at Kimball State Park. The Wood River Day-Use Area is a good place to bird watch or try your luck fishing in the icy-cold Wood River. The PCT crosses Highway 62 west of the Park entrance.

A Twisting Journey

# REGION THREE MAIN ROADS IN ORDER OF TRAVEL

**Beginning in Fort Klamath:**

**Highway 62**
From the town of Fort Klamath to the National Park entrance.

**National Park Roads**
Connecting us to highway 138 on the park's north side.

**Highway 138**
The drive from the park's north entrance to the Diamond Lake area and the stop sign at Highway 230.

**Highway 230**
We're on this road for about the equivalent of a city block. Don't blink or you'll miss the turn to…

**Road 6592/Diamond Lake Recreation Area:**
Hugs the east side of the lake and connects to the loop road around Diamond Lake.

**Back on Highway 138**
After leaving Diamond lake we'll follow Highway 138, 5.7 miles north to the Bird's Point Road.

**Bird's Point Road/Road 2610**
The road north from Highway 138 to Lemolo Lake Resort and the end of Region Three.

## Optional Roads and Other Attractions Described in Region Three

**Wood River/Historic Fort Klamath Loop**
Headwaters of the Wood River at Jackson Kimball State Park and the Wood River Day-Use Area.

**Pinnacles Road**
Interesting geological formations in the National Park.

**Optional Falls Tour**
West from the Lemolo Lake intersection, an exploration of four waterfalls along Highway 138.

# PCT ACCESS POINTS IN REGION THREE

The Pacific Crest Trail crosses Highway 62 just west of the Annie Springs (south) road entrance to Crater Lake National Park. Trail Mile 1,818.5 **Map R3.**1

Almost all backpackers on the **PCT take an alternate** to the official trail which routes hikers west of the lake's rim with nary a view of the lake itself. Stock packers are required to follow the official trail but most others follow the trail along the road and trail system established on the western rim.

The next major road crossing of the PCT is north of the Park at Highway 138, trail mile 1845.3. The total mileage between these two points via the alternate Rim Trail is just over 26.5 miles.....(a mere marathon right?).

# MAPS OF REGION THREE

The Rogue River National Forest Map overlaps the Winema National Forest Roads that are part of Region Three. Paper map geeks order your National Forest Maps online at **fs.usda.gov**.

Look for the very detailed Diamond Lake Ranger District and Umpqua National Forest maps at fs.fed.us/r6/umpqua.

Crater Lake National Park is administered by the National Park Service. Contact park headquarters at 541-594-3000 or look online for more information on the park at **nps.gov/crla**.

Find Benchmark Maps at your local sporting goods retailer. Tech geeks can download your favorite off-grid maps for your smartphone.

### Region Three map recommendations (for paper map geeks)

Diamond Lake Ranger District Map Umpqua National Forest Map

Rogue River National Forest Visitors Map

Benchmark Maps: Oregon Road and Recreation Atlas, Page 85

# REGION THREE ROUTE DESCRIPTION

This part of our journey begins at the town of Fort Klamath, Oregon and continues around the east side of Crater Lake National Park, past Diamond Lake and ends at Lemolo Lake.

Total distance is about 70 miles, allow (with several stops) 4–5 hours. If you choose to do the optional waterfall tour, set aside an additional 2 hours at least.

> **Note:** The Region Three Route is paved and suitable for any vehicle with no clearance or traction issues in good weather.

Because of the high elevations (approaching 8,000 feet) in Crater Lake Park, the North Entrance and the East Rim Road are typically closed because of snow **by late October**. The East Rim Road is closed by the Park Service no later than November 1st in any event. Road crews usually start plowing the East Rim Road in late spring with the aim of re-opening in the early summer (in typical snow years).

The road from the Annie Spring (south) Entrance Station to Crater Lake Lodge is plowed and kept open throughout the year but may close periodically during heavy snow events. The road from the Lodge to the North entrance is not maintained during the late fall into the early summer season.

All other roads described in Region Three are regularly plowed during the winter.

Be aware that the Park has begun closing the East Rim Drive to motorized traffic for one weekend in September. This usually occurs during the second or third weekend of the month, a great time to cycle or travel the East Drive by foot without being chased by a giant motor home. The West Rim Drive will remain open during this closure.

The park in downtown Fort Klamath features massive picnic tables cut from solid slabs of wood. With a population of around 20 people, it's conceivable that the entire town could be seated here at one time. The scenic Wood River winds along the eastern edge of town with the riparian area providing good habitat for birds and beavers.

# ROAD NOTES FOR REGION THREE

### Fort Klamath Town  *Elevation 4,175 feet*

From here we drive West on Highway 62 to Crater Lake National Park.

To explore the Optional Wood River Loop (described below) follow Highway 62 East.

> **Note!** The town of Fort Klamath, located on the Wood River, is just up the road from the historic army post of the same name.

This tiny community is the epitome of rural, eastern slope Southern Oregon. Open spaces and snowcapped peaks in the distance could be anywhere in the west. Squint your eyes and you could easily be looking at Colorado or Wyoming.

Several large ranches raising cattle and sheep dot the well-watered Upper Klamath Basin. It's easy to estimate that the ruminants far outnumber the humans in this area during the grazing season. Springtime comes late to the basin because of the high elevation but when it shows up…it's a glorious time of the year with crystal clear skies, snowy mountains, and knee high grass rippling in the breeze.

There are a few commercial establishments in town; a grocery store stocked with organic goods is located at Jo's Motel (see below). The nearest fuel is 14 miles east at the casino near Chiloquin and Highway 97. Gas is also available in Crater Lake Park during the warmer months.

Other lodgings available include the **Sun Pass Ranch**, a bed and breakfast and horse hotel. Contact the ranch at 541-381-2882.

The **Aspen Inn Motel** features two furnished cottages (one with a pool table) for rent along with cabins and motel rooms. The motel is very dog friendly and has a great outdoor area your furry friends will love. Contact the Aspen Inn at 541-381-2321.

**Jo's Motel** (Jo was a lady, eh?) offers lodging, camping, and a menu of organic food items in the deli. Try Robin's delicious muffins with a hot espresso.

Wanna' unplug from the 21st Century? The motel proudly advertises no phones, no TV, no kids, no pets, and no WiFi. Each neatly kept cabin-like room has its own kitchen and carport, lending it the nostalgic air of a 1960s-era family vacation motel. There's room for a couple of RVs with limited hook-ups. To contact Jo's Motel call 541-381-2234.

The wide open space around Fort Klamath presents scenes that could be almost anywhere in the western mountain states. Squint the eyes a little and you could imagine yourself in Wyoming or Montana.

## Optional Wood River Loop

### Historic Fort Klamath

**Old Fort Klamath** was located near timber and a good source of water but nowhere near the emigrant wagon roads the Army was assigned to protect from Indian attack. This military outpost with sweeping views of the Upper Klamath Basin was occupied until 1889 when it was officially abandoned.

The buildings of the fort had been crushed by 20 feet of accumulated snow the previous winter and anything left after the military's departure was carted off by local residents. The meager structures present today are reconstructions and the only historic traces left are the graves of the four Indians who were executed here for their part in the **Modoc Indian War**.

The museum is open from late May through Labor Day.

# Wood River Day-Use Area

This pleasant park located on the banks of the Wood River offers wheel chair accessible boardwalks connecting with wooden benches located strategically on the river's edge. This is a great place to picnic and a good spot for birding along the river and in the many acres of woods along the access road.

There are several picnic tables adjacent to the parking area lined by a stand of quaking aspen. Fly fishing on the Wood River is a popular (and sometimes very productive) pastime. The boardwalk takes the stroller south along the river with a good opportunity to spot waterfowl and marsh loving birds.

*The Wood River Day-Use Area is an easy stroll along the boardwalk paths. Interspersed with benches, the walkway is accessible to wheelchairs. The aspen-lined parking area has several picnic tables. Look for water-loving birds in the river riparian area.*

## Jackson F. Kimball State Park

A curious fact about Crater Lake is that it has no apparent outlet, no streams flowing out of the caldera at all. Although hard to prove, the springs marking the headwaters of the Wood River are likely coming from deep within the lake. The output of the Wood River Springs varies little throughout the year providing a steady flow even in the dry times.

The flanks of Mount Mazama, forming the rim of the ancient volcano and 1,949 foot deep Crater Lake, stand a short way northwest of the springs. The surface elevation of Crater Lake is 6,174 feet, while the Wood River Springs stand at 4,200 feet, making a difference of 1,974 feet and leaving the springs at the (virtual) bottom of the lake. Could be, we're looking at water right out of the lake itself, seeping through the porous volcanic rocks.

The park offers twelve fee sites with no water and no hook-ups. The mosquitoes can be a problem early in the season.

The good news is its only $5 to camp. Canoeists and kayakers launch here for floats down the winding Wood River.

The Wood River is very twisty (and frickin' cold) and would be a frustrating float; probably traveling 5–6 river miles to gain a mile and a half (or so) heading south. An easy float from the headwaters to the first road crossing at Dixon Road looks doable.

The trail to the **Wood River Springs** is on the right as you enter the camp. Follow the short trail upstream and discover where the crystalline waters of the Wood River actually come bubbling forth. The multiple springs flow from the jumbled volcanic rocks, forming an ice cold pool crossed by a wooden footbridge.

The park is lightly used and a great place to camp in August and September, just a few miles from Crater Lake National Park via the Dixon Road.

*A footbridge spans the Wood River at Jackson Kimball State Park. The pool in the shadows is where the Wood comes bubbling up from the rocks and begins its sinuous journey to Agency Lake.*

## Highway 62 West from Fort Klamath Town
*It's a short drive to the Park.*

The views looking south from the highway are expansive. Apparently before it was diked and drained, old Upper Klamath Lake extended to near where the highway is today during high water events. Late in the spring and early in the summer it's now ranch land and a sea of waving greenery.

## Annie Creek Rest Area

> **Note:** Before we reach the rest area we'll encounter an informational sign in a turn-out to the right. Stop and get some perspective of how deep Crater Lake is.

Located just before the Park boundary and still in the Winema National Forest, this designated rest area and sno-park has an informal camp below the rest area. Follow the dirt road leading downhill from the parking area about a block to the camp on the banks of ice cold Annie Creek. There are no services here and no fees for camping. No restrooms at the camp so just take the short walk back to the rest area to do any "resting."

## Crater Lake National Park

The immense scale and mind-twisting spectacle of the deepest lake in North America pooled with water of an impossible blue, within the collapsed caldera of one of the world's most impressive volcanoes would be very hard to express in words, so I won't even give that a shot. If you haven't seen it before, suffice to say, it'll blow you away.

*A Twisting Journey* (and its humble author) would like to take this opportunity to apologize to those map readers who've noticed that the PCT traverses the west side of the park while the Guide suggests the east side of the park as the "Main Route" (marked in RED on the Guide Map). While this may seem an egregious affront to the Guide's stated goal of providing a road trip version of the Pacific Crest Trail…

…may I point out that purists of the PCT have long bemoaned the fact that the official trail was routed well below the rim of the caldera with not a glimpse of the lake. The vast majority of backpackers avoid the official trail and choose to follow the crowds along the west side of the lake.

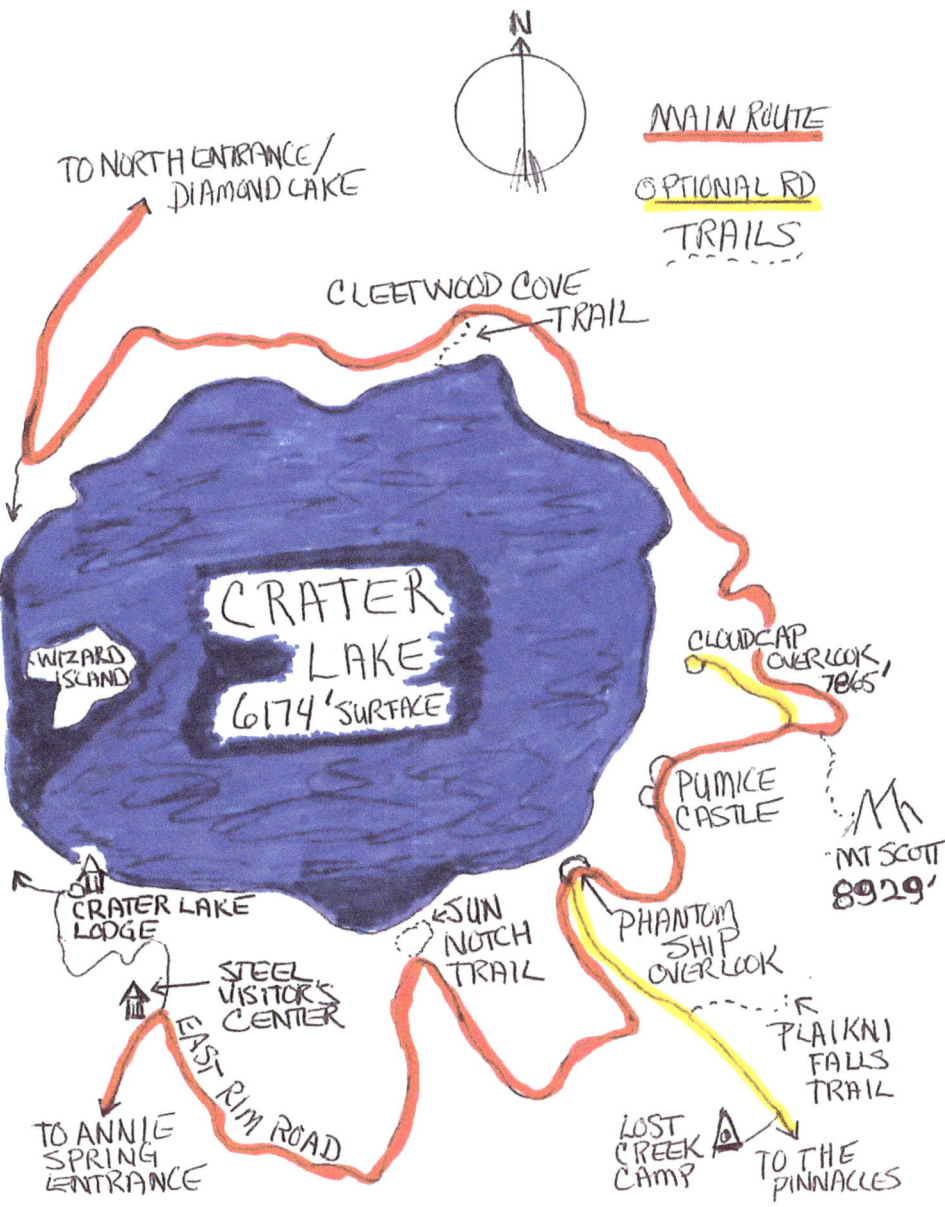

**Map R3.2 Crater Lake National Park**

*There are more than 20 turn-outs along the East Rim Road with lots of informational signs and "Oh, WOW!" views. Take some extra time to explore the Pinnacles and maybe take a hike to Plaikni Falls or the summit of Mount Scott. Cloudcap Overlook is reportedly the highest elevation paved road in Oregon. Cleetwood Cove Trail is the only footpath to the lake's surface.*

*Region Three - Town of Fort Klamath to Lemolo Lake*

Travelers with stock must stay to the lower route, backpackers have the option of hiking up to the Crater Lake Lodge and staying on or near the west rim of the caldera as they make their way north to the junction of the two trails.

While it's certainly a plus for backpackers on the PCT to experience this visual treasure, the network of footpaths (and a stint on the pavement) goes through the most heavily traveled (and very beautiful nonetheless) part of the park with attendant crowds of people and cars as part of the scenery.

If you have the time and the weather is nice, it's much better (me thinks as a wheeled traveler) to take the backroads (East Rim Drive), the way less traveled. It's probably genetic, but I like the quieter side of Crater Lake National Park.

The West Rim Road is certainly worth driving and if time is short, it's the quickest way to the park's North Junction Road and the exit via the North Entrance Station.

*The Steel Visitor Center, north of the Annie Springs Entrance, is mostly about the gift shop but there is also information about the park and a short video that is worth your while.*

## Annie Spring Entrance Station  *Elevation 6,030 ft*

From here it's 3.8 miles to the **Steel Visitor Center** and our turn-off to the East Rim Drive.

Pay the entrance fee of $30 and enter Oregon's only National Park. Long lines can form at the park entrance on summer days, it's best to get there extra early to avoid the crowds during the peak season.

The **PCT lies about a half mile west of the entrance station** along Highway 62.

Dogs are mostly restricted from trails in the National Park. Pets are allowed within 50 feet of roads and other developed areas but are not allowed in the backcountry or other trails with the exception of the Old Grayback Road, connecting Vidae Falls and Lost Creek Campground.

## Mazama Village Campground

The word village is perhaps an understatement. Operated by the park's concessionaire, this small town has 40 rooms in its motor lodge (called "The Cabins"), a grocery store, restaurant, gift shop, gas station, extensive campground with 212 sites, post office, ATM, laundry facilities and showers.

The Annie Creek Restaurant is open 7:00am until 9:00pm during the summer. Walk-in tent sites are $5 per night with car camping tent sites at $21 per night. RV sites with electrical hook-ups are $42 per night.. About ¾ of the campsites can be reserved July through September.

For further information and to make reservations, call 866-292-6720 or visit their website travelcraterlake.com.

## Crater Lake National Park HQ and Visitor Center
## East Rim Drive Intersection

From here the Main Route turns right onto East Rim Drive; its 2.9 miles to Vidae Falls.

## Steel Visitor Center  *Elevation 6,474 feet*

The buildings here are frequently featured in Southern Oregon regional weather telecasts. My favorites are always the time-lapse videos of the buildings being buried under feet of snow; the sharp lines of the buildings eventually blending into the white world of winter at Crater Lake.

The visitor center has the usual touristy stuff. There's a good selection of books and maps, hoodies and coffee mugs. Take the time to watch the slickly produced **22 minute video**. Shown every half hour, it's about a variety of subjects including recent and ongoing research projects in the park. Along with amazing underwater scenes and cool 3D effects, the video offers stunning scenic shots of the park. Narrated by Peter Coyote with a background of mesmerizing music, the video is entertaining and informative. The opening time-lapse scene of the night sky above the caldera rim is worth the price ($0) of admission.

To drive up to the caldera rim and Crater Lake Lodge from the visitor center stay left at the intersection as the road heads north (uphill). The Main Route follows the East Rim Drive from the visitor center. It's 2.9 miles to Vidae Falls.

*Vidae Falls is tiny and rather unimpressive itself but a thriving selection of plants and wildflowers run along its green and mossy course.*

## Vidae Falls

From here it's 1.3 miles to the Sun Notch parking area.

Falling over a series of rocky ledges this small but beautiful spring-fed fall tumbles more than 100 feet to a lush flower-lined pool. Be careful not to trample the fragile plant growth if you choose to explore closer.

## Sun Notch

From here it's 3.9 road miles to the Phantom Ship Overlook and Pinnacles Road intersection. Elevation 7,033 feet at the trailhead.

It's a short hike up to the notch and well worth the time. The trail is hard packed and achievable in a wheelchair with assistance. This is a great place to take first time visitors for their initial glimpse of Crater Lake.

This easy hike through several acres of wildflowers forms a loop back to the parking lot; allow 30–40 minutes.

*The enigmatic Phantom Ship formation as seen from Sun Notch. The East Rim Road approaches the caldera's rim in several spots. The hike to Sun Notch is easy and a great place to bring first-time visitors.*

## Ancient Mount Mazama

As we stroll across Sun Notch we can imagine when Mount Mazama was whole, standing thousands of feet higher than now. Before the eruptions that led to the formation of the lake, glaciers flowing from ancient (12,000-foot-tall) Mount Mazama carved a valley on its southern side between Applegate Peak and Vidae Ridge to the west and Dutton Ridge to our east.

After the summit collapsed (possibly in a matter of hours) about 7,700 years ago, this place we now call Sun Notch became a beheaded valley, itself choked with smoking debris, a notch in the rim of the resulting caldera. From the many Sun Notch overlooks gaze at the scene across the lake and marvel at the other (less dramatic) glacial notches carved into ancient Mount Mazama before the final paroxysm.

Imagine how the post eruption, rock strewn, sheer-cliffed (3,000 feet below our present viewpoint) volcanic cauldron would have looked before it cooled enough to fill with water. With steaming vents and rocks glowing red at night it must have been an awesome sight indeed to anyone brave enough to sneak a peek.

Nobody is sure exactly how long it was before the cauldron began to fill with water, but it was probably several centuries after the eruption before the lake appeared as it does today.

The views are stunning to the north where distant Mount Thielsen can be seen above the caldera rim. Various overlooks along the trail provide a good view of the Phantom Ship, anchored a thousand feet below us.

## Back on the Rim Road

We skirt south around Dutton Ridge and admire views far to the south of the Upper Klamath Basin, Pelican Butte, Mount McLoughlin and all the way south to California's Mount Shasta.

Closer up, (a few miles to the southwest) we'll see 7,709 foot Union Peak, the central plug of an old Cascade volcano.

The forests seem to blend into the horizon from this vantage point and 8,929 foot **Mount Scott** towers before us as the road bends northeast. The road turns north (with a good photo opportunity of Mount Scott) and we soon arrive at the Phantom Ship/Pinnacles Road intersection.

# Phantom Ship/Pinnacles Road Intersection

## Phantom Ship Overlook  *Elevation 6,778*

This place above the rim is also known as **Kerr Notch**, the head of another decapitated glacial valley. Those of you who took the Sun Notch hike have already spied the Phantom Ship up close.

This turnout has an interesting perspective across the lake of not only the Phantom Ship but also the western side of the caldera featuring Wizard Island and its 6,940 foot cone, 8,151 foot Hillman Peak to the left and the tiny appearing lookout atop the 8,013 foot Watchman Peak on the rim to the right of the island.

From here it's 6 miles to the optional **Pinnacles Overlook** trailhead.

**Special Note**: To skip the Pinnacles Road, see below at **Back on the Rim Road.**

## The Pinnacles Road

Head 6 miles downhill (yeah I know the sign says 7 miles) to the Pinnacle Overlook and trailhead. There's a parking area there with informational signs and vault toilets.
A trail leaves the parking lot on the south side following the bluff for more views of the impressive hoodoos and in a short way to the park boundary.

On the way to the Pinnacles we encounter Plaikni Falls Trailhead on our left.

## Plaikni Falls Trail

This easy hard-packed trail is a pleasant 2.2 mile round-trip walk through scattered forests of Mountain Hemlock and Noble Fir to an impressive spring-fed waterfall. It's a relatively new addition to the park's hiking options, opening in 2012.

The first ¾ mile or so is navigable in a wheelchair with assistance and features a view of the creek below the trail. The steeper ascent to the falls is probably not advisable for wheelchairs.

Originating at Anderson Springs at about 7,000 feet elevation, Sand Creek takes a tumble over a glacier carved ledge creating Plaikni Falls and a beautiful spray garden of wildflowers in the summer. Plaikni is a native word interpreted as "from the high mountains." Continuing downhill on the Pinnacles Road we come to Lost Creek Campground on our right.

*Showing off the calves for the folks back home, day-hiker Dennis Kruse from Anacortes, Washington at the viewing area after the grueling 1.1 mile hike to Plaikni Falls.*

### Lost Creek Campground

Located on the flats separating spring fed Lost Creek and impressively eroded Sand Creek on the other side of the road, the campground is operated by the National Forest Service and has 16 sites catering to tent campers only.

This is the only car camp in the park boundaries. Although not what you'd call scenic it's near enough to several hiking trails including the old gravel Grayback Road which is closed to motorized travel and the only substantial area in the park open to pets. With water and flush toilets it's only $10 a night.

Each site has a fire ring, picnic table and a steel bear locker. It's first come first served with no reservations taken so get there early if you expect to find an open site (and bring plenty of DEET in the early season).

## The Pinnacles

Some of these striking stone formations stand 90–100 feet tall. They were formed into more erosion-resistant rock then the ash and pumice surrounding them by the interaction of gases escaping from the hot materials buried here after the eruption of Mount Mazama.

Subsequently eroded away by wind and water in the ensuing thousands of years, the softer material has moved downhill leaving the striking hoodoos behind. Many of the spires have been found to be hollow like chimneys, apparently formed by the pressure of the escaping gases.

It's hard to express the scale when viewing a photo of the Pinnacles. The deadish looking trees at the bottom of the sandy slope stand about 60–70 feet tall and the hoodoos tower above them. Squint your eyes down real good and look at the shadows of the trees in the upper left of this pic, see the little blue patch? That's a twelve passenger van parked in the lot above the viewing point.

## Back on the Rim Road:

After leaving the Pinnacles Road intersection and heading east on the Rim Road, it's two miles to the first in a series of four overlooks at Castle Rock/Pumice Castle.

## Pumice Castle

Stop at the Pumice Castle Overlook and gaze at the orange-colored pumice rock that has eroded into shapes resembling a turreted medieval castle carved into the caldera wall. From here it's about 1.5 miles to the turnoff to Cloudcap Overlook and the Mount Scott trailhead.

## Cloudcap Overlook

It's about a mile up to the overlook from the Rim Road. At 7,865 feet elevation this is the highest road-accessible point in the park and purportedly the highest paved road in Oregon. The scene from here is, of course, stunning on a clear day. The layered structure of old Mount Mazama is very evident and the views of the surrounding country go on for a hundred miles or more.

Soak up the views across the lake then take a look up the hill behind the parking area at the gnarled whitebark pines that cling to survival in this harsh and windy environment.

*The Pumice Castle overlook not only gives us a view of the turreted orange formation embedded in the cliffs it also provides an amazing look across indigo waters to the pyramidal summit of Mount Thielsen on the southern horizon.*

## Mount Scott Trailhead

Gaining 1,250 feet elevation in 2.5 miles, the 5 miles round-trip trail to the lookout is mostly a gradual ascent with the exception of a series of switchbacks as it works its way up to the summit ridge. The trail is listed as strenuous largely because of the elevation; the trailhead is above 7,500 feet! Allow 3–4 hours for the hike. Typical snow years find the trail open in mid-July. Take plenty of water and your camera. The views of the lake from the top are best under morning light. Because of this volcano's position on the east side of the park, the amazing views up and down the Cascade Range and the endless valleys and forests to the east, combine for breathtaking scenery.

## Mount Scott

Elevation 8,934 feet, Mount Scott is the highest point in the park and the largest of the several surviving satellite cones pre-dating the eruption of Mount Mazama. These parasitic cones may have contributed to the engulfment of Mount Mazama by tapping into the magma chamber beneath the mountain, helping to evacuate the molten rock before the summit's collapse. Mount Scott's western side was heavily eroded by glaciers leaving no trace of a summit cone. Ice flowing down from ancient Mount Mazama met the obstacle of Mount Scott and gouged deeply into its northwestern slope. It's clear that this happened previous to the destruction of Mount Mazama's summit so it's apparent that Mount Scott was a fully formed volcano before the formation of the caldera and the destruction of Mount Mazama.

## Back on the Rim Road heading north

We find the **Whitebark Pine Picnic Area,** a pleasant circle of beautifully wind sculpted whitebarks with picnic tables and great views of Mount Scott. From here it's about 2.5 miles to the Lake in Legend Overlook.

## The Lake in Legend Overlook

The informational boards at this overlook illustrate the Native American legends surrounding the caldera's creation. Passed on through the generations of people who no doubt witnessed the eruption, many First People still live in the Klamath area. The National Park partners with native groups to use the park for educational and ceremonial purposes today. From the overlook its 4.0 miles to the Cleetwood Cove Trailhead.

*Mount Scott was a fully formed volcano previous to the rise and subsequent destruction of Mount Mazama. Heavily eroded, the probably extinct mountain has a hiking trail to its 8,934 foot summit and is today the highest point in the park.*

## Cleetwood Cove Trail

Only 1.1 miles to the lake? That sounds easy enough right?

Before you decide to hike this steep little beauty, spend a few minutes at the trailhead people-watching, at the pain etched into (even young folk's) faces as they climb the last few yards to the road. A reminder that the high elevation can leave you huffing and puffing.

If you do opt to stroll to the lake (and back) bring water and wear some good shoes. Swimming and fishing is allowed in the lake on the fringes of the boat launch and on Wizard Island.

The parking lot fills quickly on summer weekends so get there early if you don't already have a reservation for the boat tour. If a tour doesn't sell out, tickets can be purchased at the Cleetwood Cove ticket booth for tours leaving in 45 minutes (or up to 2 hours, 45 minutes) to allow time for passengers to walk the trail down to the boat landing. Each open motor launch holds 37 passengers and tickets are best purchased in advance to guarantee seats.

Call 1-888-774-2728 to reserve tickets.

To spend time at Wizard Island and hike to the island's cinder cone peak, you'll need to make arrangements when booking your boat reservation. Take water and food, bring a hat, sunblock and a warm rain resistant jacket.

*Wanna' talk tough? Whitebark Pine survives above 8,000 feet elevation in the Oregon Cascades. The specimens along the Crater Lake rim are subjected to the crushing weight of several feet of snow for months at a time followed by months of fierce winds and drought conditions during the summer months. Appearing bested by the battle, the gnarled trunks are eventually forced to hug the Earth. Making the most of things, the trees (some hundreds of years old) defiantly sprout green branches. Mount Thielsen in the background.*

## North Junction

From here it's about 9 miles north to Highway 138 and our turn-off to Diamond Lake.
This is the junction of the East Rim Drive and the West Rim Drive; turn south and arrive at the Crater Lake Lodge in 6 miles.

## Pumice Desert

This stark landscape also provides a dramatic view of another of the several parasitic volcanoes related to the Mount Mazama complex. The aptly (if unimaginatively) named **Red Cone** is relatively young and may have been active within the last few thousand years.

The so-called Pumice Desert is slowly being colonized by high mountain plants and animals. Although covered by several feet of snow in the winter, the porous nature of the pumice creates "desert like" conditions after the snow melts and the rain stops. What appears as barren ground from a distance on closer examination reveals a few ground hugging and drought tolerant plants making a living here.

## North Entrance Station

The North Entrance is closed no later than November 1st and is the principal way into the park for snowmobiles during the winter and early spring months. Contact Diamond Lake Resort (see below) for more information on booking snowmobile tours.

## Highway 138 to the Highway 230 Intersection

After passing the North Entrance station, we'll turn left and head west on Highway 138. Heading downhill on Highway 138 we spy Mount Bailey looming up from the west before getting a peek at Diamond Lake. After traveling about three miles we come to the major intersection with Highway 230 and the sign pointing south towards Medford. Turn Left at this intersection and head south towards Medford.
**Please read the Special Note! below.**

## Highway 230 South intersection

> **Special Note!** This is the way south to Medford. We're on this road for about a city block before turning right (west) on the Diamond Lake Recreation Road.
>
> **Special Special Note!!** Just another city block south on Highway 230 takes you to the **Mount Thielsen Viewpoin**t. Don't miss it!

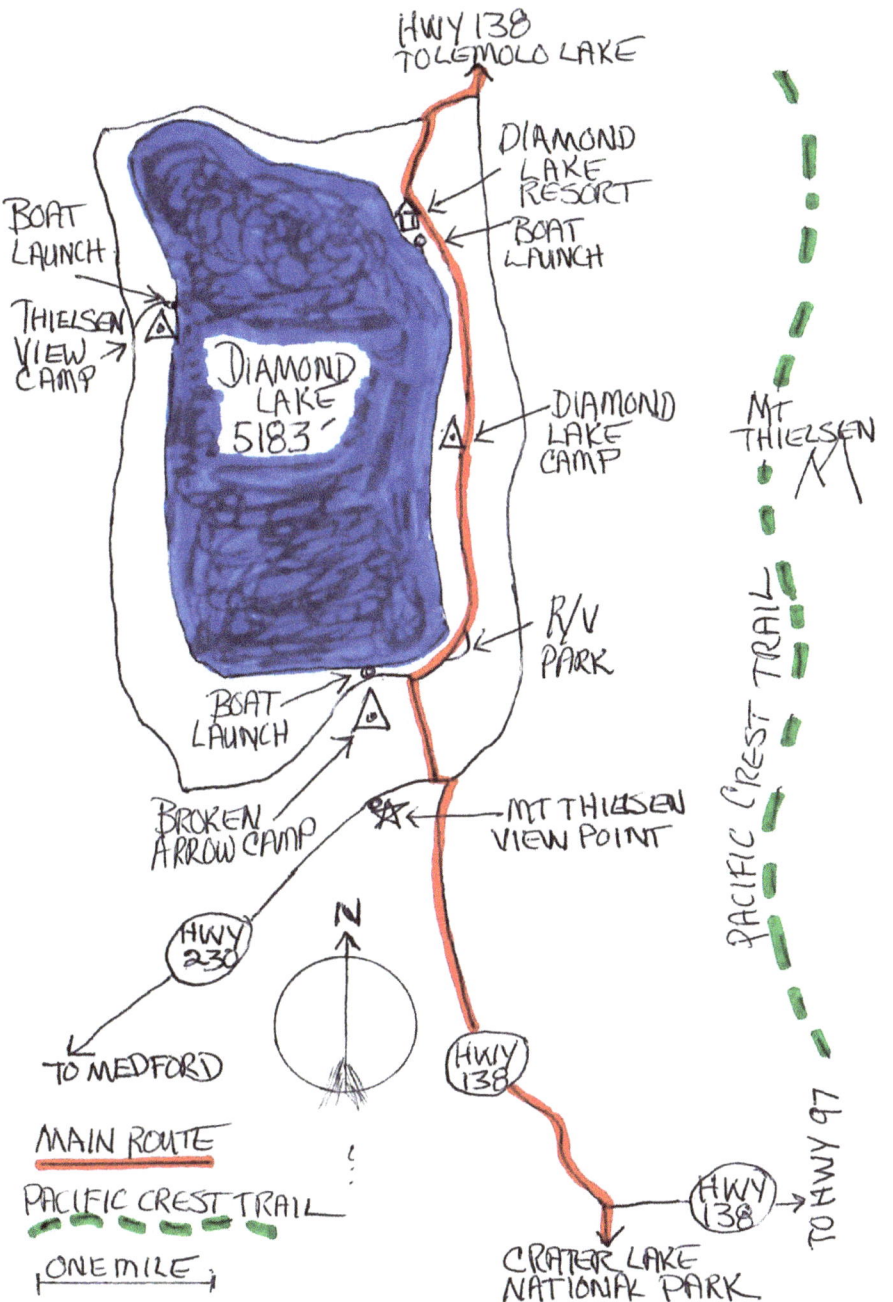

**Map R3.3 Diamond Lake**

*The "Gem of the Cascades," Diamond Lake is a natural lake and perennially one of the best fishing lakes in the Southern Oregon Cascades. Skeeters can be a problem early in the season but are done by mid-August. With several campgrounds and a paved bike/hiking path around the lake there is always something to do here.*

*Region Three - Town of Fort Klamath to Lemolo Lake*

## Diamond Lake Area

After turning off from Highway 230 we quickly arrive at an intersection where we'll keep to the right (north).

The lake covers over 2,800 acres and is about 50 feet at its deepest point.

The paved Dellenback Bike Trail loops Diamond Lake and spans about 11 miles of mostly level pavement for bikers and hikers too, just follow the bicycle icons through the campgrounds.

In the summer, stop at the South Shore Pizza Parlor along the way for food and perhaps a beer. With a great selection of microbrews, they also have a growler station, (a growler is a refillable glass container for to-go beer) and that's right…pizza!

Diamond Lake itself is largely the product of Mount Mazama and its subsequent eruption over 7,700 years ago. Pre-eruption, 12,000 foot Mount Mazama had extensive glaciers and one of these northward moving mountains of ice scooped out the valley between 9,182 foot Mount Thielsen to the east and the younger volcano, 8,364 foot Mount Bailey to the west.

When Mount Mazama erupted, it partially filled this valley with volcanic debris and formed a dike of pyroclastic material blocking the outlet of the lake's drainage. Water quickly filled the resulting depression and a shallow lake was formed. Finding an eventual outlet along the rocky ledge at today's Lake Creek, Diamond Lake "the Gem of the Cascades" came into being.

Fishing can be good and trout in the five to ten pound range are boated here annually. This natural lake and healthy food chain produces clouds of insects and aquatic critters that grow trout big and fat.

**Note:** Take warning of the clouds of insects (skeeters) that can be present here just after ice off in the late spring and early summer. These persistent devils want to include your blood in the food chain.
Hardy early season fishers and campers bring warm clothes and lots of insect repellent… August and September are the best times to camp here when un-DEET'ed flesh can be bared again.

*Mount Bailey stands guard over the western shores of Diamond Lake. The 8,376 volcano was regarded as sacred to the First People who lived in the valleys to the west and held ritual feasts on the mountaintop. There's a foot trail to the summit that gains 3,000 feet in 5 miles.*

### Mount Bailey  *Elevation 8,364 feet*

Mount Bailey stands guard over the western side of Diamond Lake.

Revered by the Native Americans who lived in the area; its name in the native tongue translates to "Medicine Mountain." Legend tells us that chiefs and medicine men held ritual feasts atop the volcano.

The trail to the mountain's summit is about 5 miles long and gains 3,000 feet, there's no water along the way. Starting out in the trees the trail reaches the tree-line after about 4 miles. The last bit to the summit is steep and rocky, look for the crater perched on the summit ridge.

During the winter the volcano is a favorite among sno-cat skiers.

### Diamond Lake Resort  *Elevation 5,193 feet at the lake*

Diamond Lake Resort (open 365 days a year) has facilities for weddings, conventions and all sorts of other events.

They have a well-stocked grocery store, post office, gas station, boat rentals and a full service marina. With a capacity of over 300 guests this is the mother of all Southern Oregon mountain lake resorts. The resort rents cabins and motel rooms and has an extensive RV park (541-793-3318).

At last count it also had three restaurants including the South Shore Pizza Parlor, the more upscale Mount Bailey Sports Grill and Lounge and the Diamond Lake Café. A full service cocktail lounge called the Diamond Room is upstairs.

The resort sponsors an annual fishing derby held in late June that attracts trout fisherman from near and far. On other summer weekends the resort holds conventions for everyone from (I'm not making this up) square dancers to radiologists.

During the winter the resort hosts sled dog races and cross-country ski races. This is also prime country for snowshoeing and snowmobiling with over 300 miles of groomed trails with races and poker runs for both. The lake is entirely on Umpqua National Forest land so it's open to shore angling everywhere. Please use courtesy and common sense when accessing the lake shore.

Diamond Lake is open year round for fishing with ice fishing usually available in the winter after the ice forms. Check your local regulations.

The nearby **Diamond Lake Corrals** offers daily guided trail rides ranging from one hour to all day and has corrals for rent with nearby camping for those bringing their own horses. Contact Diamond Lake Corrals at 541-793-3337 or 541-297-6095 or on the web at diamondlakecorrals.com.

## Campgrounds in the Diamond Lake Area

Call 541-793-3310 or 541-498-2531 for Forest Service Campgrounds information or take a look at **recreation.gov**.

## Diamond Lake Campground

This humongous campground has 239 fee sites laid out in linear fashion stretching almost two miles along the eastern shore of Diamond Lake.

The various designated loops in the road layout use up a good portion of the alphabet starting with the letter "A" and ending with "M." More than half of the campsites can be reserved by calling 877-444-6777 or on the web. All other sites are first come, first served.

The campground has two boat ramps and a fish cleaning station. There are showers, flush toilets and RV dump station. Its $16 to camp inland, lakefront sites with views of Mount Bailey and afternoon sun are $6 extra.

## Broken Arrow Campground

Only half the size of Diamond Lake Campground, Broken Arrow has a measly 117 fee sites located inland from the south shore of the lake; $15 for family sites. It's about a half mile to the South Shore Day-Use Area and boat launch.

Each campsite has tables and fire rings and some can accommodate trailers up to 35 feet. There are flush toilets and showers accessible to wheelchairs. Most sites are first come, first served with reservations available for some group site.

Mosquitoes can be an issue at any of the Diamond Lake campsites, especially early in the season but for whatever reason, the winged demons can be really bad at Broken Arrow.

## Thielsen View Campground

They don't call it Thielsen View for nothing, you know. With 60 fee sites, water, boat ramp, vault toilets, and killer views of Mount Thielsen this heavily used, improved campground located on the northwest shore of the lake has nice waterfront exposure among the trees. It's $15 to camp here.

Thielsen View Campground is located across the lake from the resort along the 4795 Road. Heading north along this road we come to the junction of the Resort Road and the **Diamond Lake Gas Station.** This is the best place to gas up if you're following the Guide through Region Four. The station is about two city blocks above Diamond Lake Resort and a city block downhill from Highway 138 and our turn-off northbound to Lemolo Lake intersection.

*Thielsen View Campground features (Surprise!) killer views of Mount Thielsen. Diamond Lake is a natural lake, sitting in a glacially scooped basin. Year after year this lake is among the best trout fisheries in the Oregon Cascades.*

## Lemolo Lake Intersection  *Elevation 4,535 feet*

The main route leaves Highway 138 at this intersection and travels north to Lemolo Lake Resort/KOA. Those not wishing to take the Falls Tour, look below at **Lemolo Lake Intersection Continued.**

## Optional Falls Tour

Continue west on Highway 138 from the Lemolo Lake Intersection. Who doesn't love a waterfall? This short stretch of Southern Oregon's Cascades, spanning the area between Lemolo Falls and Tokatee Falls contains six significant waterfalls, each with its own personality. Two of the falls (Lemolo and Warm Spring Creek) are described in Region Four while the other four are described in this optional side-trip from the Lemolo Lake turn-off.

*One of two waterfalls on the Clearwater River, the sparkling beauty of Clearwater Falls is a very short walk from the parking lot. Perhaps the least visually exciting of the four falls described in Region Three of this book, the informational signs at the viewing area help paint a more interesting picture.*

Region Three - Town of Fort Klamath to Lemolo Lake

## Clearwater Falls

The first falls we encounter as we drive west on Highway 138 is on the Clearwater River. As the name implies, the waters of this river are exceedingly clear. Just a mile or so above the falls, the river emanates from pure springs flowing from a jumble of lava. The viewing area for the falls is a very short walk and wheelchair accessible. Adjacent to the parking area there's a pleasant picnic area and informational signs.

## Whitehorse Falls

Also on the Clearwater River this pleasant fall is a very short walk from the parking area and has access to the pools below. The Whitehorse Campground (5 sites) is nearby.

*Whitehorse Falls is just a short walk from your car. Of the four falls described in this section of the book, this one is easiest to access for those with disabilities. A full sensory experience, it's noisy here with lush, moss draped rocks and logs lining the splash pool. The picnic area adjacent to the parking lot and overlooking the falls provides an opportunity to linger.*

The trail to Watson Falls is draped in rainforest splendor. Following the course of the creek through the rocks, the trail is short but somewhat strenuous. The trail splits near the top providing a short loop back to the parking area.

## Watson Falls

From the parking area it's about 0.3 miles to the falls viewing area.

The trail is rather strenuous and immediately heads uphill following Watson Creek through lush glades and past sparkling pools. Typical of the western High Cascades, this area gets about 80 inches of precipitation annually. Look for wildflowers of all descriptions among the massive trees and moss covered rocks below the spray pool.

The falls push over a sheer columnar basalt cliff and descend 293 feet, making it the tallest waterfall in Southwestern Oregon. Heading down from the viewing area there's an alternate trail that follows the other side of the creek, making a short loop back to the parking area. There are informational signs in the parking area with some beautiful photos of the falls taken during winter along with general information about the local geology.

*Watson Falls reveals itself through the lush undergrowth. Views of the falls are somewhat limited by the clouds of spray generated by the nearly 300 foot waterfall.*

# Tokatee Falls Trailhead

The trail to the falls overlook is about 0.3 miles from the parking lot.

As we pull into the parking area it's hard to ignore the huge wooden pipeline (called a "penstock") adjacent to the pavement. Made of redwood and banded together with metal staves, the penstock channels water under gravity pressure (squirting out in places) downhill from here to power turbines creating electricity. It's all part of Pacific Corp's hydroelectric project on the North Umpqua, an extensive operation with 8 dams and multiple generating stations.

The trail follows the North Umpqua downstream (west) and after negotiating hundreds of steps (both uphill and downhill) you'll arrive at a wooden platform overlooking the falls. The platform is perched on a steep slope and wraps around a huge tree, giving it the feel of being high up in a tree house with an exquisite view.

Soak up the awesome scene of the North Umpqua River as it falls over a series of basalt ledges before launching into space 80 feet above the splash pool.

*The parking area at Tokatee Falls is adjacent to Pacific Corp's penstock. With ice-cold water squirting out in places, the penstock provides a nice shower or car wash after your hike to the falls.*

*The viewpoint for Tokatee Falls is high above the North Umpqua River. Water flowing over the solid basalt has carved a multi-tiered slot through the rocks. A view through the massive trees presents a dramatic scene.*

## Lemolo Lake Intersection Continued

Back on the Main Route, we'll head north on the Birds Point Road for about three miles to the intersection with the 2614 Road.

## 2614 Road Intersection

From here we continue north on the 2610/Birds Point Road towards Lemolo Lake Resort and the end of Region Three.

The road to our right (east) is the East Lemolo Lake Road and goes to East Lemolo Lake Campground, Inlet Campground, Crystal Springs, the road to Timpanogas Lake and the Windigo Pass Road, all described in Region Four.

Staying on the 2610 Road it's about a mile to Poole Creek Campground.

## Poole Creek Campground

With 59 fee sites, Poole Creek campground is located on the southwest shore of Lemolo Lake. This improved campground is much quieter than anything you'll find on more popular Diamond Lake but it can be busy on summer weekends. With water, vault toilets, garbage and recycling service, a boat ramp and a beautiful day-use area, it can be downright peaceful here (and relatively bug-free) in late August and early September.

Heading north on the 2610 Road as we leave Poole Creek Campground we quickly encounter an intersection to our left (west). This is the 3401 Road and leads to the trailhead (on the 840 Road) to beautiful **Lemolo Falls,** described in Region Four. Staying north on the 2610 Road we soon arrive at the turn-off to **Lemolo Lake Resort** and the end of Region Three.

## End of Region Three

The end of Region Three finds us in western Oregon near the headwaters of the mighty Umpqua River at Lemolo Lake.

*In Region Four we begin at Lemolo Lake and end here, at Odell Lake and Willamette Pass. This view from Shelter Cove resort shows the ski-runs carved out of the mountain above the ski resort located at the pass. This is also the beginning of the companion book in this series, A Twisting Journey Continues which describes a new adventure as we follow the PCT through northern Oregon to its end at the Columbia River.*

# Region Four
## *Lemolo Lake to Willamette Pass*

*Some campsites on Lemolo Lake are either a short walk-in or boat-in only. The reservoir is located high in the Upper Umpqua drainage and part of the Pacific Corp hydroelectric project. Lemolo Lake is the anchor point for our exploration of the Region Four area.*

"I seemed to be obsessed by the spirits of wanderlust,
and they all but deprived me of my senses.
The guardian spirits of the road beckoned,
and I could not settle down to work.
The moon and the Sun are eternal travelers.
Even the years wander on.
Every day is a journey and the journey itself is home."
– *Japanese Poet Matsuo Bashō*
From the poetry collection *Narrow Road to the Interior* (1702)

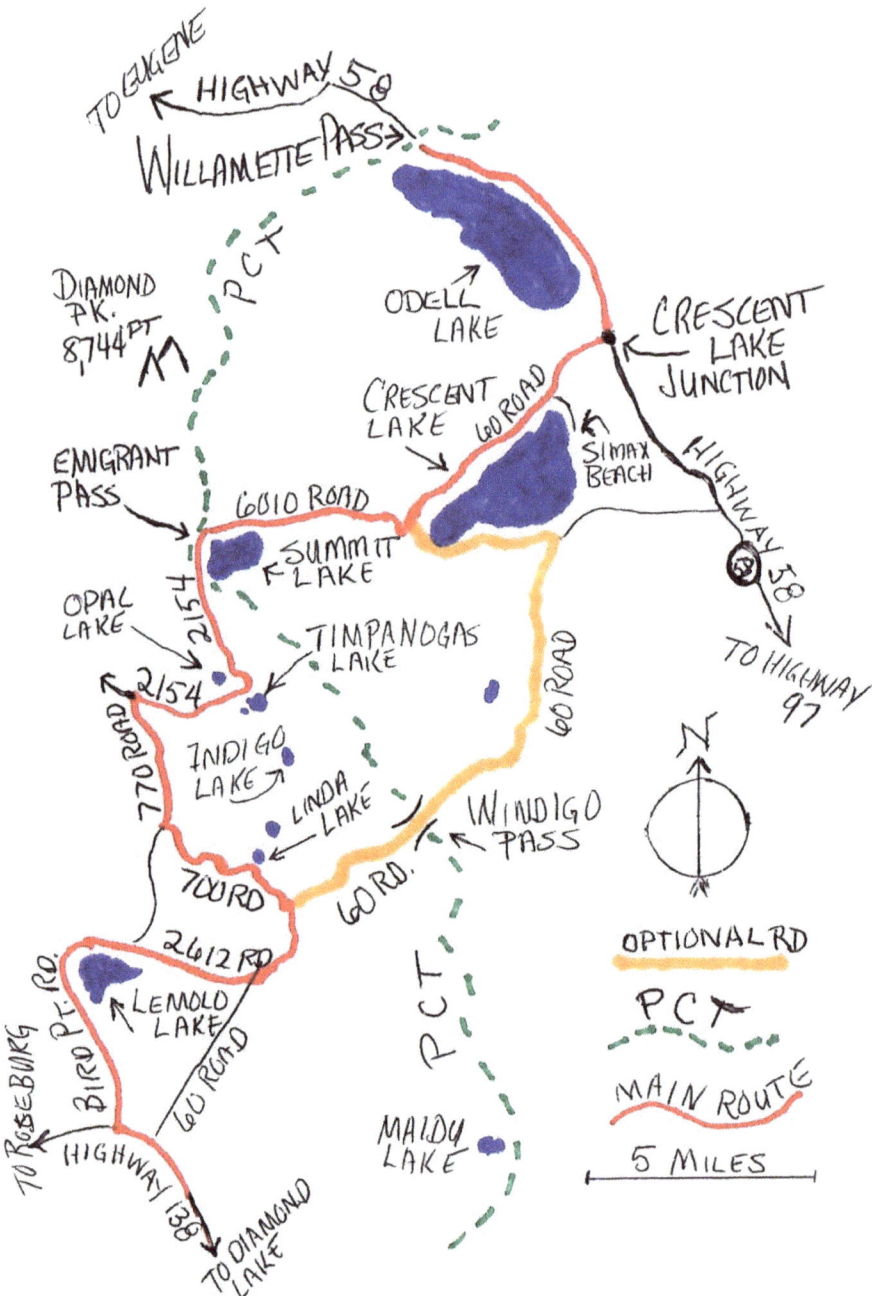

**Map R4.1 Lemolo Lake to Willamette Pass**

*Beginning at Lemolo Lake we continue our twisting way northward to Willamette Pass. The only part of this road route requiring clearance and 4-wheel-drive (or at least your rugged sport UTE) is the challenging 6010 Road connecting Summit and Crescent Lakes. Seeking some solitude? The back country of Region Four is some of the quietest territory in Western Oregon.*

# REGION FOUR MAIN ROADS IN ORDER OF TRAVEL

**Beginning at Lemolo Lake:**

**2610/Birds Point Road Intersection**
(North from Highway 138) The paved road to Lemolo Lake Resort and KOA.

**60/Windigo Pass Road**
We're on the 60 Road for 2.3 miles to our turn at the 700 Road. (The **PCT crosses the 60 Road** at Windigo Pass).

**700 Road**
The good gravel road past Linda Lake.

**770 Road**
The gravel road over the Calapooya Divide to the 2154 Road.

**2154 Road**
Good gravel road to Timpanogas and Opal Lakes.

**6010 Road or NF 398 on Google Maps**
The GNARLY road past Summit Lake to Crescent Lake.

**60 Road**
The paved road around Crescent Lake to Crescent Junction.

**Oregon Highway 58**
The highway to Odell Lake and Willamette Pass.

## Optional Roads and Other Attractions Described in Region Four

The two short hikes to waterfalls described in this region are the biggest attractions for the traveler in Region Four.

There are other short hikes to out-of-the-way lakes and a hike to the summit of Cowhorn Mountain for the more ambitious.

# PCT ACCESS POINTS IN REGION FOUR:

**Windigo Pass**
   Trail mile 1,875.8, elevation 5,821 feet

**Willamette Pass**
   Trail mile 1,905.4, elevation 5,088 feet

Most backpackers take an alternate to the PCT that begins just north of the Windigo Summit (the Oldenburg/Nip and Tuck Lakes Trail).

Day or multi-day hikers may wish to consider the "official" trail. Although it may be dry(er) (especially in the late season) there is much less traffic for those wishing more for solitude than camaraderie. The official PCT skirts Summit Lake and the 6010 Road, described later in Region Four.

## REGION FOUR ROUTE DESCRIPTION

This part of our journey begins at Lemolo Lake, heads north over the Calapooya Mountains, skirts Crescent and Odell Lakes and ends at Willamette Pass. The Main Route travels past four additional lakes and through some of the least traveled areas of the central Cascades. The optional roads lead to two waterfalls near Lemolo Lake (with short hikes ) and for low clearance vehicles, across Windigo Pass to Crescent Lake.

Lemolo Lake Resort is the last place to gas up before Crescent Lake Junction. Total distance is 50-65 miles. It's not many miles but the 6010 Road (NF 398 Rd) can eat a lot of time. Allow 5-6 hours with several stops.

Most of the Region Four route is paved. There's about 20 miles of dirt road (not plowed in the winter) regardless of the route chosen. The gravel then dirt road across Windigo Pass is **suitable for any vehicle** with reasonable clearance when it is snow-free.

The Main Route also traverses about 20 miles of dirt road, all of it improved and suitable for most vehicles with the exception of the 6010 Road/NF 398 Rd around Summit Lake.

The 6010/NF 398 Road connecting Summit Lake with Crescent Lake should only be attempted by high clearance vehicles. (See **Map R4.1**)

Contact the Crescent Ranger Station at 503-433-2234 for roads in the Deschutes National Forest, or the Ranger Station in Oakridge at 503-782-2283 may have some info. Call the Diamond Lake Ranger Station at 541-498-2531 for road information in the Umpqua National Forest.

**Maps recommended for (***paper map geeks***) Region Four:**

Umpqua National Forest

Diamond Lake Ranger District

Deschutes National Forest

Benchmark Maps, Page 73

The **Umpqua National Forest, Diamond Lake Ranger District and Deschutes National Forest** maps are available online. Look for **Benchmark** maps at your local outdoor retailer or order online.

# ROAD NOTES FOR REGION FOUR

### Lemolo Lake Area:

It's a pretty little (out of the way) spot among the pines with Mount Thielsen framing the eastern skyline. Who could ask for more?

Lemolo Lake is part of Pacific Corp's hydro-electric project on the North Umpqua Basin. Formed by a dam on the upper river the 415 acre lake provides fishing and recreation opportunities.

Served by four National Forest Campgrounds and a resort, the lake is a more sedate alternative to Diamond Lake in the summer. There are boat ramps at the resort, East Lemolo Lake Campground, and Poole Creek Campground.

There are a few informal camps along the northern shore of the lake that offer camping right on the lake and a couple of boat-in sites are available elsewhere on the lake.

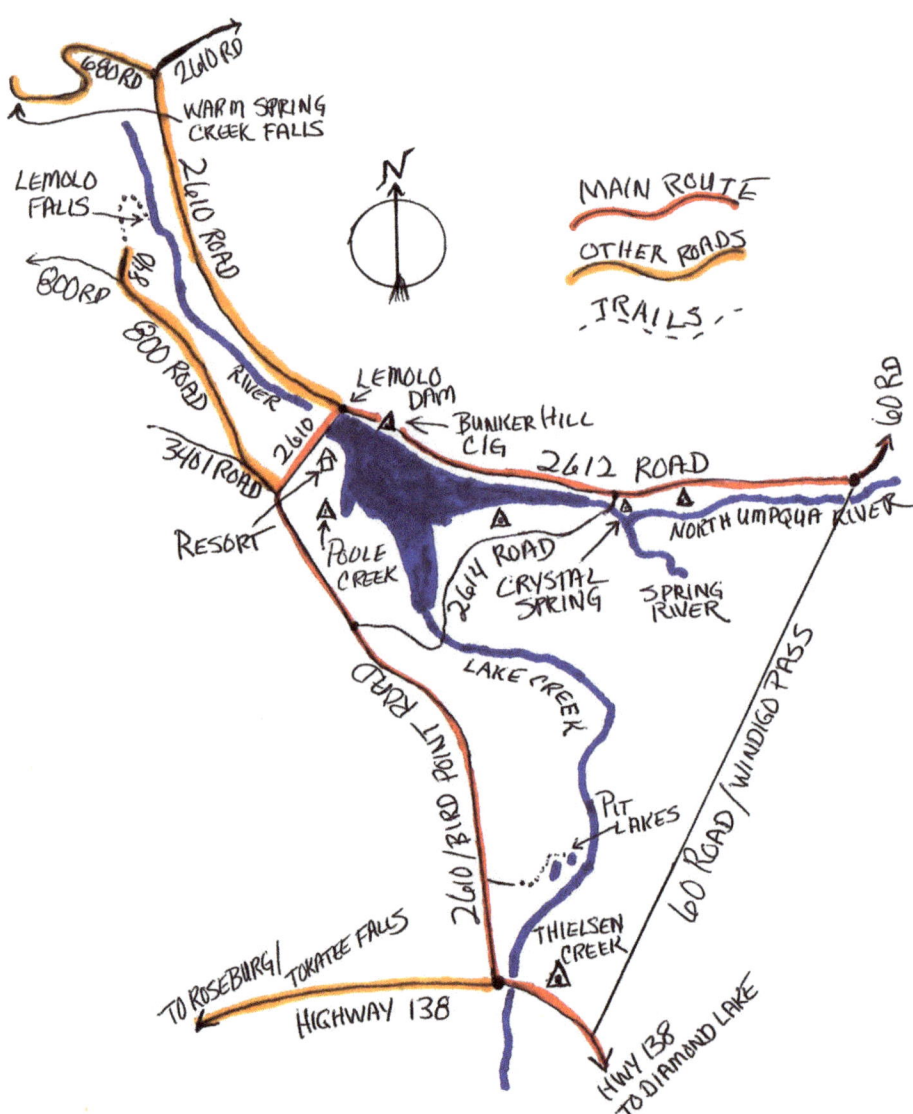

**Map R4.2 Lemolo Lake Area**

*Before we head off into the hinterlands of Region Four, we'll take a look at some of the interesting features of this section of Oregon's Cascade Mountains. There are six significant waterfalls within a reasonable drive from the Highway 138 intersection with the Lemolo Lake turn-off. Lemolo Lake is a popular alternative for fishing and camping to the more crowded Diamond Lake.*

*Colorful wooden carvings welcome visitors to the Lemolo Lake General Store. The laid-back resort recently changed hands beginning an association with KOA and an energetic couple from Kansas. The new partnership plans an expansion of campground, marina and R/V amenities.*

## Lemolo Lake / Crater Lake North KOA
*2610 Birds Point Road  541-643-0750  lemololake@koa.com*

Expect a relaxed atmosphere when you're checking in at the Lemolo Lake / KOA. The venerable resort operation recently changed hands with owners Jim and Anita Hudson moving from Kansas to take the reins. Providing new energy, their affiliation with KOA means many new and upgraded facilities, especially in the RV park. The resort offers a few tent sites with one lakefront.

Plans are also in the works for a new playground for children of all ages, and a dog park. Located near the dam on the northeast side, the lake is the star of the show at Lemolo Lake Resort.

With a store, boat rentals, marina, cabins and an RV park the resort caters to fishermen in search of the big brown trout (30 inches plus) that inhabit these sparkling waters and those who seek some peace and quiet. Grab your fly rod and fish from a float tube in the inlets early in the morning for a chance at the big brownies.

Fishing for rainbow and kokanee is available from the resort's docks. Swimming and boating of all sorts including pontoon and fishing boats, canoeing, paddle boards and kayaking fill in the summer season.

Like Lemolo Lake itself, the pace is laid back and quiet, especially during the late part of the season. The resort and the surrounding National Forest campgrounds can get busy in August (before school but after mosquitoes).

After Labor Day, the rhythm slows and September usually brings sunny and warm weather with fewer bugs and people around the lake. The store has a selection of camper's supplies and fishing gear. The owners and staff are happy to offer advice and show you the various set-ups commonly used to fish the lake.

The RV park has sites with full hook-ups from $46 per night. The cabins rent from $150 per night. There are also four motel rooms available from $100 per night.

## Trails in the Lemolo Area

**Lemolo Falls Trail:** So what's your idea of the perfect waterfall? Perhaps it's the tropical version with beautiful wildflowers, ferns, and towering rocky cliffs? Well strap on your daypack and check these falls out on a midsummer morning. Sure the temp might be in the 50's but the ferns, beautiful wildflowers, and rocky cliffs are there… The North Umpqua trail follows the north side of the river and provides views down into the canyon near the falls but **there's no trail down to the falls from that side.**

Instead, take the **3401 Road** (marked in yellow on **Map R4.2**) to the **800 Road**, turn right (north) on the **840 Road** to the trailhead parking lot. It's about a mile from the parking lot to the end of the trail and the falls.

The trail descends along an old roadbed to an ancient car camp, complete with ancient picnic table. From there the trail descends the river's canyon in one long switchback, arriving at a good view as the full force of the North Umpqua River plummets more than 100 feet before rejoining the river below. The formal trail ends here but those more nimble (or foolish) can scramble over the slippery, moss covered rocks to the foot of the falls.

*A lush, moss covered splash pool awaits the hiker below spectacular Lemolo Falls. The hike to Lemolo Falls covers about a mile, one-way. The falls are noisy and the mists from the spray can feel very nice on a hot summer day.*

**North Umpqua Trail:** Unlike the north/south nature of the PCT, the North Umpqua Trail follows the east/west direction of the Umpqua River.

Beginning in the early 1970's, trails advocates promoted the construction of a trail that would connect the Lower North Umpqua with its ultimate source at Maidu Lake, high in the crest of the Cascades next to the PCT.

Completed in 1997, the **79 mile trail** takes hikers, fishers, cyclists, and horsemen through several stands of old growth trees, a hot spring, and past waterfalls galore. There are 12 main trailheads providing access to trail segments varying in length from 3.5 miles to over 15 miles.

**The Swiftwater Trailhead** on the lower river near Glide, stands at just over 800 feet elevation. As the path heads east it steadily gains elevation topping out at 6,000 feet near **Maidu Lake.**

**The White Mule Trailhead** near Lemolo Lake stands at 3,920 feet. Head west along the **"Dread and Terror"** segment to **Umpqua Hot Springs** and you'll travel about 13 miles while losing 1,200 feet elevation.

Travel east 6.3 miles from White Mule and you'll gain 360 feet elevation to the next **trailhead at Kelsay Horse Camp.** From the horse camp the path crosses into the Mount Thielsen Wilderness and ends at the PCT near the Cascade Crest at **Maidu Lake**, about 10 miles from Kelsay Horse Camp.

**Warm Spring Creek Fall Trail:** Hike this short, wheelchair friendly trail and find a beautiful waterfall cascading over a row of basalt columns. Warm Spring Creek flows well even in the heat of summer. The creek has carved a niche through the solid basalt and presents a striking scene among the massive trees and mossy rocks. The viewing area is above the steep sided creek bed with no practical way down to the base of the falls, so enjoy your picnic there.

To drive to the trailhead from Lemolo Lake Resort, head north on the 2610 Road across the dam. Past the dam the road splits with the 2610 Road turning left (west ) (marked in yellow on Map R4.2) and the 2612 Road turning right (east) towards Windigo Pass.

Stay left on the paved 2610 Road for about 3 miles to the first major intersection on the left. Here we'll turn left (west) on the gravel 680 Road. The road switchbacks as it heads downhill and in about 2 miles we come to the small parking area and marked trailhead for Warm Spring Creek Falls on our left.

It's an easy walk on the packed gravel path to the viewing area at Warm Spring Creek Falls. The dramatic scene of the creek flowing through a notch carved in the basalt columns is worth the short hike. There's no easy way down to the splash pool from the viewing area. Is the water even remotely warm? Nuh-uh. **Map R4.2**

## Campgrounds on Lemolo Lake:

### Bunker Hill Campground

Located above the north shore of Lemolo Lake, this small campground has 6 fee sites and is best suited to tent campers and those with small RVs. Turn-around space is limited so this camp will not accommodate big trailers. The campground has vault toilets and water. There's no road connection to the lake here but a short hike leads down to water's edge and a pleasant beach when the lake's full.

### East Lemolo Campground

There's an official boat launch here, but it's best suited to smaller boats. The boat launch is more useful when the lake is full. A few of the campsites have waterfront where a boat can be brought to shore. Some folks with bigger boats launch at Poole Creek or the resort and tie-up here. East Lemolo has 15 fee sites, vault toilets and water. It's $10 to camp here.

### Inlet Campground

Above this campground several springs contribute their waters to the North Umpqua as it flows into Lemolo Lake. The Spring River and Crystal Springs provide ice-cold waters to the reservoir regardless of the season. The *kokanee* (land locked salmon) follow their primal urges and flash spawning colors during their September and October foray into Spring River. Waiting below at the confluence, the big browns gulp up any love-drunk kokanee that dance their way. This is also the time fisherman target the trout where the North Umpqua merges into the lake. Inlet has 14 fee sites, vault toilets, no boat launch. It's $10 to camp here.

## Lemolo Lake to Timpanogas Lake  Map R4.3

The roads connecting the two lakes can be navigated by most any car. There are the usual potholes and washboards to contend with but no clearance or traction issues. I've even driven my trusty old Japanese sedan from Lemolo to Timpanogas and back with no problems (in good weather and snow-free roads).

Our connection to the 60 Road and the continuation of our route is the 2612 Road. From the Resort Road we head north across Pacific Corp's dam. The north end of the dam has a small parking area with great views of Mount Thielsen. There are some informational signs here and a path down to the lake's edge. Fishing can be good from the shore here especially in the early season.

The continuation of the Bird Point Road across the dam brings us to a three-way intersection and a stop sign.

From the stop we'll turn right and follow the 2612 Road to its intersection with the 60 Road. But before we get to the 60 Road we'll encounter the intersection with the 700Road to our left and the turn-out to our right and Crystal Springs.

## 700 Road Intersection and Crystal Springs

The gravel 700 Road angles away from the pavement and heads steeply up hill. If your goal is to get to Timpanogas Lake (and points beyond) this is one of your options.

I don't include this route in my descriptions because you would miss Linda Lake and besides, the mileage being about the same, the eastern part of the 700 Road and the continuation of this book's descriptions is a better road. I mostly mark this intersection to draw your attention to Crystal Springs.

## Crystal Springs

As we depart the lake we find the intersection of the 700 Road and the tight turn-around at Crystal Springs. Located east of **Inlet Campground** and just below the 2612 Road, a single informal campsite adjacent to the springs allows access. The multiple, ice cold springs flow from the hillside below and are major contributors to the North Umpqua.

To the southeast, the much bigger springs forming the headwaters of the **Spring River** comes bubbling forth from the rocks and joins the nearby North Umpqua River.

We leave the Lemolo Lake area behind as we travel east on the 2612 Road to its intersection with the 60 Road. At the intersection we'll turn onto the improved gravel road leading to our turn-off at the 700 Road.

## 60 Road Intersection

### Special Note about the 2612 Road and 60 Road Intersection!
The Main Route heads north on the 60 Road for only 2.3 Miles before turning west on the 700 Road and heading to Linda Lake. For those following the Main Route and not driving across Windigo Pass continue the description below at **Heading Northwest on the 700 Road.**

Heading up the 60 Road, look for the turn-off to the 700 Road to your left. The 700 Road may not be signed but it's a wide, gravel road heading uphill across the road from a large road sign. The **sign at the turn-off** states: **Windigo Pass 5.**

*Jeffrey's Shooting Star (dodecatheon jeffreyi) is a member of the primrose family and named after botanist John Jeffery (1826-1854) who also described the Jeffery Pine (Region Two). A member of the extensive primrose family, the flower is commonly found along stream banks and mountain meadows. This perennial ranges from Alaska to California and east to Montana and Colorado. In June and July, the riparian area along the North Umpqua is a great place to look for Jeffery's Shooting Star.*

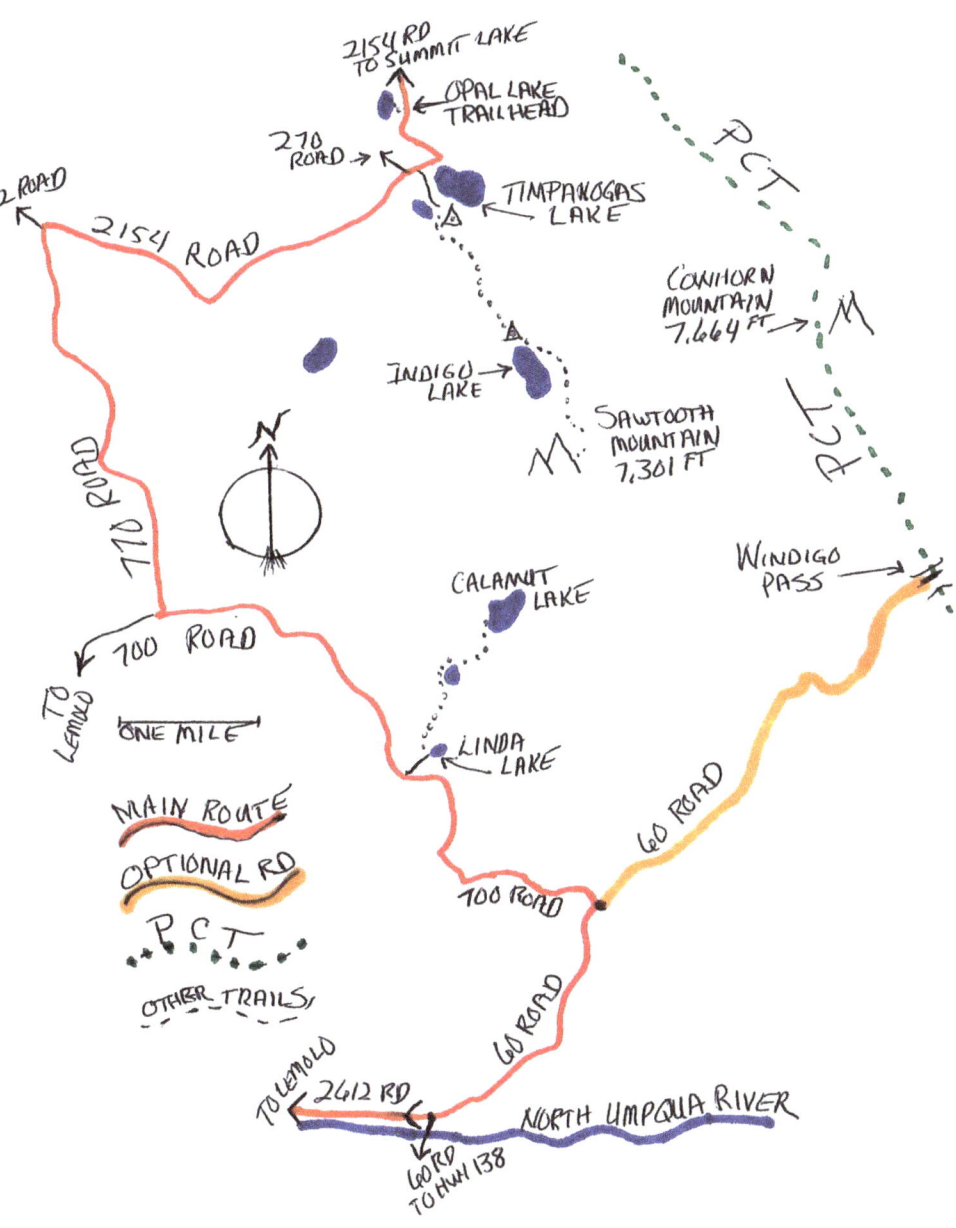

**Map R4.3 Lemolo area to Timpanogas Lake**

*Some nice day-hikes to trout lakes in this lonely part of the Cascades. Don't expect to see a lot of people in the region north of Lemolo Lake. The 2612 Road and 60 Road intersection is at the bottom of this map.*

While the road across Windigo Pass is the optional road and best for low clearance vehicles, it's also **a busy crossing of the PCT**. I've not done it yet but this would be a **great place to set-up a trail angel station**...just sayin'.

Many hikers take an approved alternate to the formal trail there to avoid a particularly dry section of the PCT. **Trail 3845** begins after a short walk downhill north of the summit on the 60 Road and goes past a couple of lakes and a spring fed creeklet.

### Optional 60 Road across Windigo Pass  *The PCT crosses here.*

> **Note!** Windigo Pass Road crests the Cascades at over 5,800 feet and is not plowed in the winter. The pass is typically closed by snow ( at least to wheeled vehicles) from November through late spring or early summer. From the intersection of the 2612 Road and the Windigo Pass Road it's a total of 16 miles to the stop sign near Crescent Lake. If you choose to take this optional road you will stay on the 60 Road to its intersection with Highway 58 at Crescent Lake Junction.

It's probably safe to say that of all the improved road passes in the Cascades, Windigo Pass is the second least traveled (after Griffin Pass described in Region Two of this guide). Like Griffin Pass, the Windigo Road 60 essentially goes north/south but divides Western Oregon from Eastern Oregon. From the south near Lemolo Lake the 60 Road heads north and takes travelers from The Umpqua drainage into the Deschutes River drainage near Crescent Lake.

The road is washboarded and heads steadily uphill as we leave the North Umpqua and travel northeast on the 60 Road, attaining the summit in about 7.5 miles. At the Windigo Pass summit, elevation 5,824 feet, we **intersect the Pacific Crest Trail.** From the summit, the 501 Road heads south (uphill) and in a very short way comes to an unmarked campground. With fire rings and a couple of picnic tables this spot is used by PCT hikers, horse campers, and car campers alike.

As we head downhill on the 60 Road it becomes narrower and mildly rutted but any car (with reasonable clearance) will do; a half mile below the pass we come to another trailhead on our left. This is the 3845 trail (Oldenburg Lake trail), used by PCT hikers as an alternate to the main route mostly because the "official" trail is waterless for many miles north. After leaving the trailhead the road widens and becomes less steep as it makes its way north to the stop sign, 8.6 miles from Windigo Pass where we'll turn left (west) and continue on the 60 Road.

After turning west we arrive in one mile to the turn off at Contorta Campground (see description below), located on the south shore of Crescent Lake. The 60 Road continues around Crescent Lake and to the town of Crescent Lake Junction.

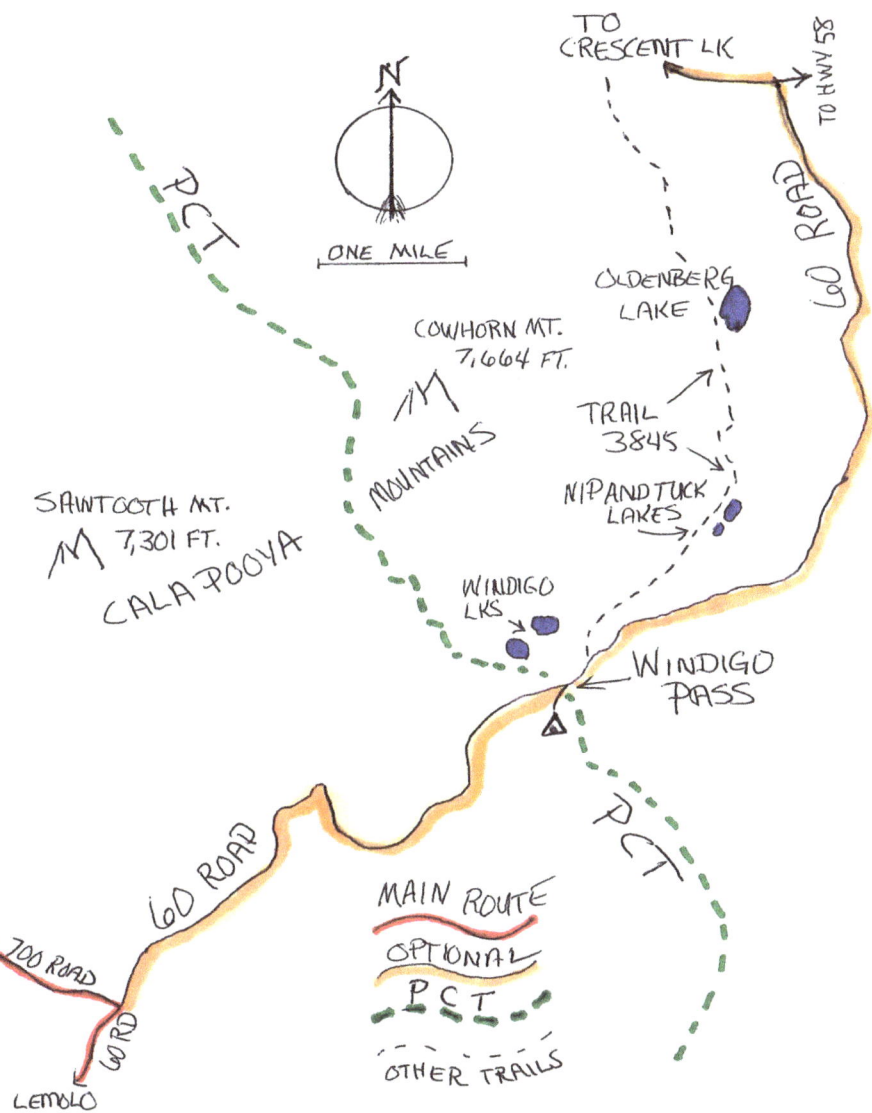

**Map R4.4 Windigo Pass Area**

*Many hikers on the PCT part ways with the "official" trail at Windigo Pass, following the 3845 Trail. The summit elevation is 5,824 feet and seldom snow-free before early summer in snowy years. The optional 60 Road is best suited for low clearance vehicles or for those who wish to avoid the very rough 6010 Road from Summit Lake to Crescent Lake.*

*Region Four - Lemolo Lake to Willamette Pass*

## Heading Northwest on the 700 Road

Leaving the 60 Road behind, the 700 Road begins to head uphill to its intersection with the 770 Road. After traveling uphill about two miles, keep an eye to the right for the 740 Road. The secondary 740 Road is rutted but almost any car can make it the short way to Linda Lake.

## Linda Lake Campground

This tiny campsite (only one spot with a picnic table) is waterfront on Linda Lake, elevation 5,560 feet. The lake covers about four acres and is surrounded by tall trees. There's an outhouse (of sorts) adjacent to the turnaround.

**Trail 1494** leaves the campground and takes the hiker to a pair of larger lakes. The trail starts at the campsite and heads uphill (north) to **Lake Charline.**

After skirting shallow Lake Charline the trail continues uphill and in about 1.5 miles arrives at 18 acre **Calamut Lake,** elevation 5,890 feet. There's a nice campground at the south end of Calamut with a view of Sawtooth Mountain, 1.5 miles to the north. Calamut is basically landlocked with no outlet; it's occasionally stocked with brook trout.

Back on the 700 Road we continue northwest for about three miles to our turn-off at the 770 Road.

## 700 Road and 770 Road Intersection  *Elevation 5,659 feet*

We turn right (north) on the 770 Road. This is a three way intersection and the 700 Road continues west from here and back down to Lemolo Lake.

This intersection is on the edge of a large forest fire that burned west of here in the recent past with many dead, standing trees evident in the distance.

## Heading North on the 770 Road

On this road we cross the Calapooya Divide and enter the Middle Fork Willamette (pronounced wil-LAM-mit) drainage. After leaving the 700 Road intersection, the 770 road continues north and uphill to its crest at the intersection with the 2154 Road.

It's here that the waters divide and we leave the mighty Umpqua River drainage behind as we travel north.

This pass has no official name so I nominate "Calapooya Gap." The 770 Road officially ends here and becomes the 2154 Road as we continue north and head down-hill on the 2154 Road.

The road to our left (west) is also confusingly labeled the 2154 Road but ignore the sign (and this very rough road) and stay on the main road heading downhill.

Consult **Map R4.1**

*California Tortoiseshell butterflies (nymphalis californica) can be found in abundance in Oregon's southern Cascades. Some years there are population explosions filling the air with exuberant adult butterflies. Hikers often remark on their encounters with veritable clouds of these insects. The appearance of dozens or even hundreds of these guys at mud puddles is a remarkable sight. The larval stage feeds almost exclusively on members of the wild lilac family of plants (Ceanothus), this adult opened its wings and posed for the camera.*

## Calapooya Gap  *Elevation 5,618 feet*

The 770 Road officially ends here and becomes the 2154 Road as we continue north and head down-hill on the 2154 Road. The road to our left (west) is also labeled the 2154 Road but ignore the sign (and this very rough road) and stay on the main road heading downhill.

The geographically significant **Calapooya Divide** is a roughly 60 mile long ridge that runs east/west and divides the Umpqua River from the Willamette River. Named after the First Americans who inhabited the area; the ridge begins in the west near I-5 and culminates in the east at 7,664 foot Cowhorn Mountain where the Umpqua, Willamette, and Deschutes Rivers divide.

After leaving Calapooya Gap, the road heads downhill and in about a mile we come to the three-way intersection, with the 362 Road to our left (west) and an information sign indicating Summit Lake and Timpanogas Lake to our right (east). From here we **head east (turn right) on the 2154 Road.**

*Looking west from Calapooya Gap we see the rocky slopes of Warm Spring Butte, one of the Calapooya Mountains.*

*Gazing northwest, the headwaters of the Middle Fork Willamette River are flanked by snowy Diamond Peak to the north. The west side of the divide is wetter and supports thick forests and dense undergrowth. It was late in the year of 1853 that the "Lost Wagon Train" descended into this "Green Hell" expecting to find a new road.*

### 362 Road Intersection

If the informational sign is intact and not SUBAR (shot up beyond all recognition) the decision is clear, turn right and head east on the 2154 Road toward Timpanogas Lake.

After leaving the 362 Road intersection we get glimpses of the fabled **Middle Willamette Valley** to our left as we continue east on the 2154 Road towards Timpanogas Lake. In about 2.5 miles we encounter a beautiful mountain pond/lake next to the road, one of the many tarns dotting this part of the Central Oregon Cascades.

This is a great spot to turn off the road and look for bird life (herons and other waterfowl) or let the dog go for a swim. The road begins to bend north and a half mile past the pond; we come to the **three way intersection with the 270 Road** heading north (downhill) and the 2154 Road turning east and uphill.

## 2154 Road and 270 Road Intersection  *Elevation 5,286 feet*

This wide spot with a view of the Middle Willamette Valley is also a "heli-spot," a landing zone for helicopters to ferry firefighters and equipment in fire season or medi-vac should the need arise.

Keeping right on the 2154 Road we'll find the entrance to Timpanogas Campground is just uphill and to the right on the 399 Road. The 2154 Road heads north past Timpanogas Lake to the Opal Lake trailhead and on to Summit Lake.

Before heading down to the lake, stop here and gaze down into the misty headwaters of the most fabled river in Oregon folklore. The waves of Euro American pioneers and adventurers had heard of the famous climate and deep soils of the **Willamette Valley.**

Most of the earlier emigrants braved the treacherous Columbia River Cascades to deliver them to the fabled land, and many lost their lives along the way.

A toll road (the **Barlow Road**) was later developed to move wagons across the Cascades south of Mount Hood delivering travelers to the Sandy River and Oregon City. Beyond the money charged, the road certainly took its "toll" on man and beast as well. The country was rugged, the weather iffy, with the muddy, winding road crossing many raging streams.

Many travelers dreamed of a more direct way into the upper Willamette Valley and a way was hacked out of the jungle covering the western slopes of the Cascades and lower Middle Fork Willamette Valley by volunteers working from the west beginning in the early 1850's. The way was to be a "free" road with no fees, and so the idea of the **Free Emigrant Road** was born.

Acting on bad information, the first wagon train attempting to cross the "road" encountered little more than blazed trees marking the way with huge logs of fallen trees crisscrossed like pick-up sticks blocking their path. With beasts dying and people starving, the folks in the settlements around Eugene mounted a rescue.

The survivors of the infamous **"Lost Wagon Train"** nearly doubled the Euro American population of the Upper Willamette Valley in 1853.

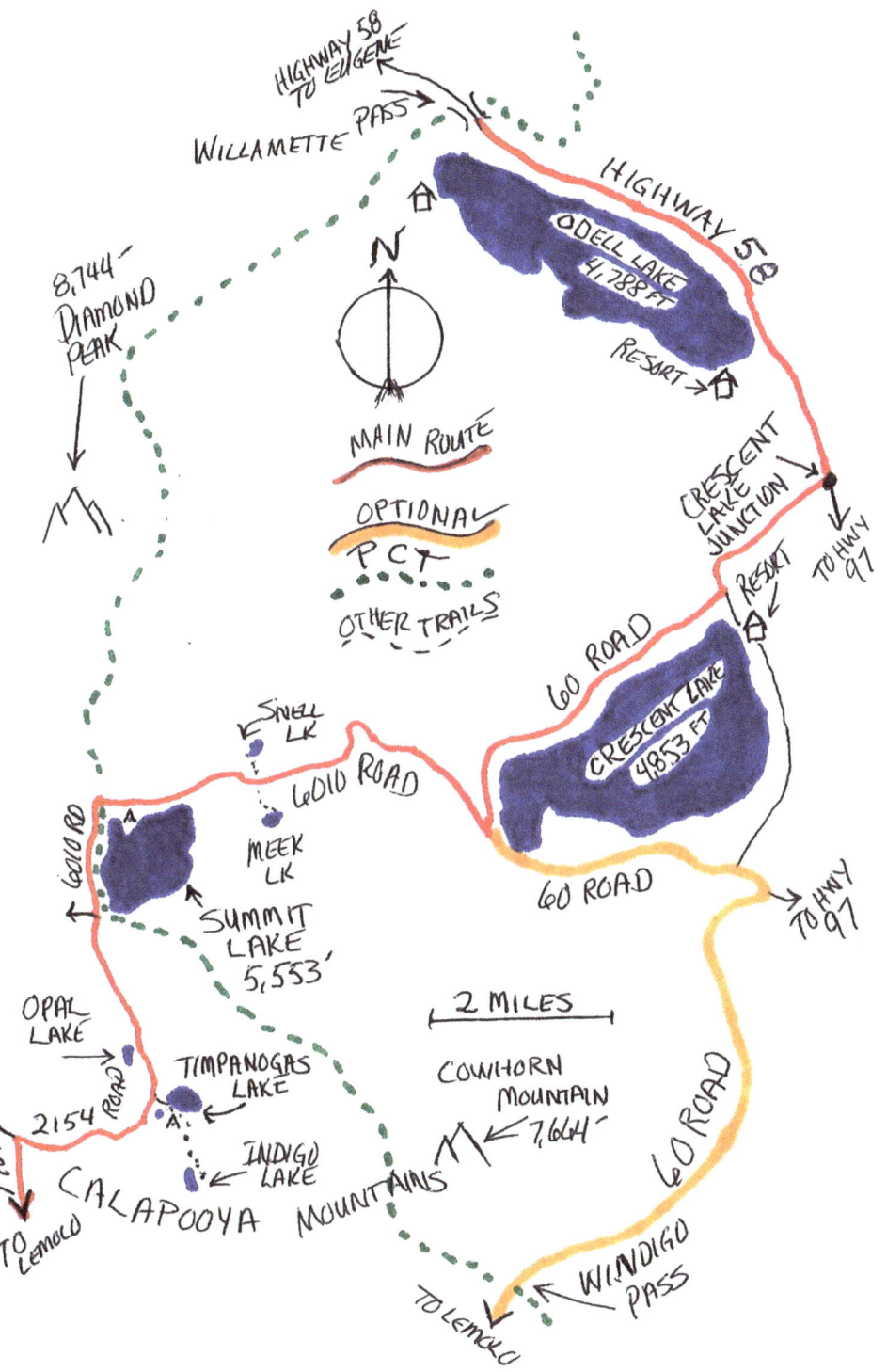

Map R4.5 Timpanogas Lake to Willamette Pass

## Timpanogas Lake and Campground Elevation 5,280 feet

Mile-high Timpanogas Lake is generally recognized as the source of the Middle Fork Willamette and attracts fisher people and solitude seekers. There are several pot-hole lakes scattered about the general area. Little Timpanogas is a very short distance from the main body. June Lake and Indigo Lake are fairly short hikes from Timpanogas.

As you enter the campground you might not even notice the large drainage pipe you will drive over. This flow of water beneath the road is officially the beginning of the mighty Middle Fork Willamette River.

There's pump-handle water past the entrance to the **Timpanogas Lake Campground.** The boat-launch is shallow so don't expect to launch your yacht here. It's possible to get small boats on the lake if you don't mind doing some wading, no motors allowed.

You can't make reservations for this isolated campground but no worries, it's rare to see big crowds in this country. Right next door is lovely **Little Timpanogas** which has no formal campsites. Both lakes hold brook trout and cutthroat.

Sawtooth Mountain is a member of the Calapooya Mountains and part of the view-shed from the Timpanogas Lake Shelter. The smallish Timpanogas Lake Campground is just across the lake from the shelter. A couple of trails connect here with the "Start O Willamette Trail" beginning at the cabin.

Across the lake from the campground is the **Timpanogas Lake Shelter.** Only available by reservation, this sturdy little structure is very rustic with a dirt floor. It comes with great views, a sleeping platform, table, chairs and a wood stove for heat. The shelter is $60 per night as of this writing.

## Indigo Lake Trailhead

Too busy for you at Timpanogas Lake? There's a trailhead adjacent to the campground that connects with **Indigo Lake** and June Lake. It's about a mile and a half with an elevation gain of over 700 feet to Indigo.

There is a pleasant campsite with a view of **Sawtooth Mountain** at Indigo among the trees on the south shore. Sitting in a glacier scooped basin, the south end of Indigo Lake abuts a massive rock slide emanating from the steep, rocky north slope of Sawtooth Mountain. Sawtooth is part of the Calapooya Mountains and sits near the eastern end of that range. Cowhorn Mountain, two miles east of Sawtooth is the last of the Calapooya Mountains.

The trail continues past Indigo Lake and ascends to the ridge line just east of Sawtooth Mountain and the junction of the Windy Pass Trail. Turn right at the junction and walk another short mile to the trail's high point. A side trail heads steeply up to the summit of Sawtooth Mountain and a rocky scramble will get you to the top.

Look back the way you came and admire the pretty indigo waters of Indigo Lake below and Diamond Peak to the north. Look a mile and a half to the south and spy 18 acre Calamut Lake and beyond that, Mount Thielsen.

## Timpanogas Lake to Willamette Pass Map R4.5

### Options from here:

If you choose not to attempt the very rough 6010 Road connecting Summit and Crescent Lakes and still wish to get to the Willamette Pass area, you can choose to take the 2154 Road from Summit Lake to Oakridge (on Highway 58) or, turn around and head back to Diamond Lake where you can hookup with Highway 138 heading east to Highway 97 and its intersection with Highway 58 (the Willamette Pass Highway).

The road from Summit Lake to the town of Oakridge covers about 40 miles, the majority of which is paved. The last seven miles around Hill Creek Reservoir is maddeningly winding but paved.

Still in for the complete tour? I salute you!

Leaving Timpanogas Lake behind, we turn right out of the campground and head east on the 2154 Road. The road gains some altitude as we bend north and we soon arrive at the Opal Lake trailhead.

## Opal Lake Trailhead

Their may be an unburned hiker symbol bravely standing when you arrive but otherwise the trailhead is unmarked; look for a turn-out on the left (west) side of the 2154 Road shortly after leaving Timpanogas Lake. You can glimpse the pretty little lake from the road. Unfortunately, a wildfire in 2018 burned the big timber down to the shoreline.

Still worth the short walk, the path heads down an old road bed and quickly arrives at the lake shore. There is a small informal camp here and another camp (with remnants of an old picnic table) located along the shore to the south. Show up here in the early summer and you'll no doubt have the 10–12 acre lake to yourself (and a zillion skeeters). Remember, late August and early September usually brings better weather and fewer flying devils. It's close enough to the road to drag your inflatable boat or even wheel your kayak down the footpath for some floating fun. Fishing can be good late in the season with a scattering of (mostly small) brook trout in the lake; look for huckleberries along the shoreline in September.

## Back on the 2154 Road

After leaving the Opal Lake Trailhead, we continue north to the intersection with the 6010/ Summit Lake Road. Along the way to the Summit Lake turn-off the road continues uphill to its crest, a little more than a mile north from the Opal Lake trail.

This high point is the actual crest of the Cascades where the road crosses over another unnamed pass. There's no sign here (as of 2019) but we cross into eastern Oregon at this point and **enter the Deschutes National Forest (and the Deschutes River drainage)** and leave Douglas County as we enter Klamath County.

## 2154 Road and 6010 Road Intersection  *Elevation 5,663 feet*

We turn-off the 2154 Road and head north on the 6010 Summit Lake Road. **Note!** The 6010 Road may be shown as the **NF 398 Rd on Google Maps.**

The 2154 Road continues west from this 3-way intersection and arrives at Highway 58 (Willamette Pass Highway) near the town of Oakridge in about 40 miles.

**OK, you're officially in the middle of nowhere.**

Look around, this is what it looks like. Kinda' dusty and quiet I'm betting. The 6010 Road and the Main Route heads north and downhill intersecting the (official) **Pacific Crest Trail** in 0.3 miles.

Remember that most PCT hikers take a different route to the east of Summit Lake so this stretch of the PCT is lightly traveled. The road is deeply rutted in places. There's a small, informal campsite here on Summit Lake shared by hikers and car campers alike.

With big views of Diamond Peak four miles to the north and an interesting looking island off shore, this is a pretty place indeed. The road doesn't touch the shore of the big lake but it would be feasible to launch a kayak or canoe here.

Just over a mile from the crossing of the Pacific Crest Trail the road arrives at Summit Lake Campground There are no fees, 3 sites, and a boat launch suitable to very small boats.

The 6010/NF 398 Road to the campground (1.4 miles) is negotiable by most any vehicle (as long as the driver has some courage) in good weather. Past the campground the 6010 Road becomes rocky and steep in places; I don't recommend the road past the campground for any vehicle with clearance issues.

*The view from the PCT crossing at Summit Lake reveals snowy Diamond Peak to the north. It's feasible to launch a small boat here with a tiny sheltered cove and a slot through the brush. There are several campsites in the trees shared by car campers and hikers alike. Few through hikers on the PCT come this way, following a trail alternate from Windigo Pass. The road past the Summit Lake Campground is extremely rugged and not suited to passenger cars.*

*Mormon Fritillary (Speyeria mormonia) can often be spotted in the dry woodlands of the Cascades' east side. This butterfly has morphed into several subspecies covering a vast geographic area. Noted by its fairly large size and orange color, males can be often found at mud puddles where they work the mud for salts necessary to mating.*

## Summit Lake and Emigrant Pass

Amazingly beautiful Summit Lake, elevation 5,433 feet, is situated at the top of the Deschutes drainage and therefore has little in-flow. Probably fed by springs, this more than 500 acre crystal clear lake maintains a pretty steady level throughout the summer months.

Launching from the campground, the lake has many surprises for the paddler with hidden inlets and islets scattered about east of the boat ramp. During the late spring and early summer melt-off, Summit Creek holds water and drains into Crescent Lake.

The rest of the year the lake has no visible outlet as water sinks below the porous volcanic rocks and disappears along stretches of the creek and then, like a magic act, re-appears downstream.

Like Waldo Lake to the north, Summit Lake is incredibly clean and clear. With no silt and little algae to cloud the surface, visibility is almost unbelievable with the lake bottom clearly seen to depths exceeding 50 feet, under calm conditions. Unfortunately for fishermen these conditions do little to support aquatic animals like fish.

The lake does support a small fishery and an occasional lake trout to 7 pounds has been reportedly landed. Otherwise, mostly brook trout and kokanee are hooked here.

The Pacific Crest Trail parallels the western shore of Summit Lake as it makes its way towards **Emigrant Pass.** Located just above the tiny Summit Lake Campground on the northwestern shore, 5,521 foot Emigrant Pass is where the infamous **"Lost Wagon Train"** of 1853 crossed the Cascade Crest headed for the Willamette Valley.

Later, the trail became the **Central Oregon Military Road**, upgraded in 1865 and 1866 to facilitate the movement of men and supplies during the Indian Wars of that era. The wagon road was re-built in the 1930's to accommodate modern vehicles and it doesn't look like much effort has been made to maintain it since then.

Deeply rutted, I don't recommend the Emigrant Pass road for anything but high clearance four wheel drive vehicles.

*Stunning views of snow covered Diamond Peak are offered up at Summit Lake. The lake waters are incredibly clear with no silt and little algae to cloud the surface.*

## 6010 Road heading east to Crescent Lake

**Note:** The 6010 Road is not recommended for passenger cars past the Summit Lake Campground.

At the three-way intersection above the campground there's a sign showing the way to Crescent Lake. It's a slow go on the 6010 Road past the Summit Lake Campground. Big rocks and steep hills present obstacles all the way to its end at Crescent Lake, about 6.2 miles from the campground.

Large sections of this road are built on the old wagon road circa 1850's and I imagine the wagoneers of that time cursed the rocky road then as I do now. Things probably aren't that much better today.

Look for a turn-out along the south side of the 6010 Road, 1.3 miles from the campground. A good sized, arm of the lake lies a short way down the hill from here with a feasible campsite along the shore.

Back on the road to Crescent Lake we soon encounter the trailhead marking the Meek Lake/Snell Lake Trailheads.

## Meek Lake/Snell Lake Trailheads

Haven't seen another human all day but still looking for some solitude? If you're not big into the company of your fellow man or woman, the country surrounding these four beautiful lakes offers that and more. Many more shallow ponds and small lakes can be found nearby that are attractive to both bird and animal life.

Speaking of animal life, all of this beautiful, soggy alpine environment also means gobs of breeding grounds for mosquitoes and therefore, gobs of mosquitoes in the early season. I know I've said this before but, don't forget the DEET and the head-net while exploring these environs early in the season.

There are trailheads on both sides of the road. The trailheading south crosses normally dry Summit Creek and winds through open woods before arriving at a bluff overlooking surprisingly deep Meek Lake. There's a small, informal campsite on the 10 acre lake with nothing more than a fire ring.

It's about 1.4 miles to Meek Lake from the 6010 Road. The trail heading north into the Diamond Peak Wilderness from the road goes to three lakes with Farrell Lake, on a short side-trail to the right off the main trail, being the first hikers will encounter. There's a campsite here and on Snell Lake.

The trail turns west from Farrell Lake and soon arrives at Snell Lake. Tiny Cornett Lake lies to the north and east of Snell Lake. This is the southern edge of the Diamond Peak Wilderness with the next road about 10 miles north as the crow flies. It's about 1.4 trail miles to Snell Lake from the road.

**Back on the 6010 Road**

The rocky/gnarly way continues eastward and in about four miles from the Meek Lake Trailhead, and after one last ugly, downhill stretch of ruts and rocks, we arrive at a stop sign (really?) and the blessedly paved 60 Road.

Now don't get me wrong...I may bad-mouth this section of the 6010 Road but there is a lot of beauty around the edges here.

Beautiful fields of wildflowers early in the year are worth the beating all by themselves. Quiet, and plenty of wild country also means lots of places for wild things. Stop and prop the folding chairs in a likely spot like a creek side or next to a pond, grab the binoculars and look around. Be patient and I guarantee you'll spot something interesting.

*Pussypaws are deep rooted and can survive droughts and wildfires. Found along the 6010 Road.*

## Crescent Lake Area  *4,853 feet at the spillway.*

Crescent Lake is huge and covers more than 5 square miles. This big glacier carved lake is over 250 feet deep. Although it's a natural lake, there is a small dam raising the water level slightly and Crescent is used for irrigation. Consequently, lake levels are typically drawn down during the summer months.

There are three Forest Service camps at the lake, three group camps, a horse camp, four day-use areas, a comfortable resort, and a dog beach. If one of those doesn't work for you there are many hiking and cycling opportunities in the area too.

Some monster lake trout live in these waters and fishers with boats fight the persistent winds to troll the deep drop-offs and ledges where the big mackinaw live. Kokanee fishing can be very productive. Wind surfers, jet-skiers and bigger sailboats love the wind and waves and hot summer afternoons usually see them on the water.

The Simax area on the northeast side of the lake has two pumice beaches with sunny exposures and a group camp. The improved day-use areas both have vault toilets and cost $5. The north beach allows dogs and the other doesn't. There are two more **day-use areas** on Crescent's southwest shore, **Tandy Bay** and **Tranquil Cove**. Bald eagles are attracted to area streams during the fall spawning action.

## Crescent Lake Resort
### 541-433-2505

Located at the northern end of the lake where Crescent Creek begins its journey east to the Little Deschutes River, the resort has a café (try the fish tacos) and a bar. While sitting next to the outdoor fireplace, you can sip a cold one on the pleasant patio overlooking the lake.

The resort has a small store and a fuel dock. The restaurant has a full bar with a breakfast buffet. The marina rents jet-skis, fishing boats, kayaks, paddle boards and water bikes. The resort also rents mountain bikes, and during the winter, snowmobiles.

They offer 18 cozy cabins for rent that are spread along the shore and among the trees. Dogs are welcome for an additional fee.

*A calm morning is bad news for sailors but great for early morning photographers. This is the view from one of the cabins at Crescent Lake Resort. Afternoons in the summer brings more reliable winds to Crescent and Odell Lakes.*

*Tranquil Cove Day-use Area features picnic tables scattered in the woods, vault toilets, a wide beach and a place to launch small boats. 7,644 foot tall Cowhorn Mountain is on the horizon.*

## Campgrounds in the Crescent Lake Area:

### Contorta Point Campground and Group Camp

The name of this campground is derived from the scientific name for the lodgepole pine, *pinus contorta*, twisted pine.

This twisty tree is ubiquitous to the highly fire prone eastern slope of the Oregon Cascades and thick stands surround Crescent Lake. The campground has 12 fee sites and a boat launch (suitable for small craft only). The wide beach and pleasant day-use area draws the recreation crowd on summer weekends with watercraft of all descriptions lining the pumice shoreline. Water skiers, wake boarders, and jet skiers dominate the water while sunbathers and stick-chasing dogs rule the beach.

The group camp section of **Contorta Flats** has 4 fee sites and can accommodate trailers to 40 feet.

### Spring Campground

With 68 fee sites and a boat launch arrayed along the southern shore this campground attracts plenty of campers on hot summer weekends. Many of the sites have waterfront access when the lake is full. Later in the season as the lake is drawn down for irrigation a beach appears.

The paved roads in the camp are ideal for families with bicycles and the beach area is great for kids and dogs.

### Crescent Lake Campground

Located on Simax Bay across from the resort, the campground has 46 fee sites and a boat launch. With the resort a stones throw away, the campground has easy access to the store and restaurant too.
There are three yurts available for rent, one of which is wheelchair accessible. Pets are not allowed in the yurts at this time.
Call 1-877-444-6777 to reserve the yurts year-round.

The trail to Fawn Lake and a connection to the PCT in the Diamond Peak Wilderness is adjacent to the campground. With an elevation gain of 800 feet the trail to more than 40 acre Fawn Lake is about 2.5 miles long from the campground.

*The beach at Contorta Point with Diamond Peak on the horizon.*

*Yurts are wheel chair accessible and a cozy alternative to bulky RVs or off-season tent camping. Currently, pets are not accepted.*

### Windy Group Camp

It's down a pretty rough road to the campground. Nonetheless it's typical to find some massive 5th wheelers rounded up like a wagon train there. This camp has but one site and can accommodate trailers to 60 feet (people really have 60 foot trailers?).

### Whitefish Horse Camp

Located in the forest on the southwest corner of Crescent Lake, Whitefish Horse Camp has 19 sites, many with corrals. Most of the sites can accommodate trailers to 40 feet. Whitefish Creek Trail 42 takes riders and hikers north from the camp to Diamond View Lake and the heart of the Diamond Peak Wilderness. The camp is on the opposite side of the road.

### Simax Group Camp

Simax Group camp has 4 sites and can accommodate trailers to 30 feet. Located on the northeast side of Crescent Lake the camp is close to the resort and the Simax Beach day-use area.

*The Mountain House Kitchen is quickly becoming Crescent Lake Junction's place to eat. The food is fresh and comes in huge portions. I tried the battered, deep fried chicken tenders. Yumm!*

*Located along Highway 58 in Crescent Lake Junction and with hitching posts out front, Manley's invites you to tie-up the (iron) horse and wash away the trail dust with a cold one.*

## The Town of Crescent Lake Junction

The small town of Crescent Lake Junction lies two miles north of Crescent Lake along Oregon Highway 58 and serves as the commercial hub for Crescent and Odell Lakes. There's gas, groceries, a post office and an extensive deli at the **Odell Sportsman Center**. T**he Willamette Inn** provides motel accommodations in town.

A little over a mile east of the junction on Highway 58 you'll find the **Crescent Creek Cottages** with kitchens, showers and a laundry. As advertised, beautiful Crescent Creek runs behind the cabins with access for fishing or splashing about on a hot day. Pets are welcome for an additional charge. There's room for RVs with full hook-ups from $30 a night. The cottages are fully furnished and reasonably priced. Call Crescent Creek Cottages at 541-433-2324.

For a cold beer and decent food (broasted chicken is their specialty) try **Manley's Tavern** in Crescent Lake Junction. The interior of the bar is cavernous with pool tables and comfortable seating.

## Highway 58 Heading West

As we leave Crescent Lake Junction it's a straight shot to our next turn at Odell Lake. It's a little over one and a half miles to our turn-off to the left (south) to the East Access Road and Odell Lake Resort.

## Odell Lake Area

Odell Lake is one of the largest natural lakes in the Oregon Cascades. More than five miles long and covering more than 3,500 acres, this glacier carved lake is almost 300 feet deep at the east end near Odell Creek Campground. The lake is situated on the eastern side of Willamette Pass and surrounded by towering trees. At an elevation of 4,788 feet, the winds can be fierce, churning up whitecaps and usually blowing fishermen off the lake by mid-day.

Windsurfers, jet-skiers, and sailors of all descriptions take advantage of the reliable afternoon winds here. More than thirty creeks and many springs keep the lake level at a near constant level throughout the summer and fall. Look for bald eagles and osprey at the creek mouths in the latter part of fall, harvesting the fish spawning in the shallows. Trapper Creek is a good spot to look for eagles.

The lake is served by four drive-in campgrounds and a boat ramp. There are two resorts on the lake, **Odell Lake Lodge** on the east end and Shelter Cove on the west end.

Fishing can be very good at Odell. Lake trout (also called mackinaw) were first stocked in 1902 and are now a self sustaining population. The state record lake trout was taken from Odell in 1984, weighing in at a prodigious 40lbs and 8ozs. Most macks caught in the lake average about 10lbs. Some impressive rainbow trout to more than 20 inches are boated here annually.

There's also an abundant supply of kokanee (land locked salmon) that are preyed upon by the big lake trout and bald eagles. First stocked in the lake in the early 1930's, their average length is about a foot with larger fish occasionally hooked. At this time fishermen are being encouraged to catch and keep up to 25 kokanee per day to reduce the population.

*Odell Lake Lodge is located on the east end of five mile long Odell Lake where Odell Creek begins. Founded in 1902, the resort is apparently the oldest such operation in Oregon.*

*A paddle boarder near Odell Creek takes advantage of calm conditions on Odell Lake.*

## Odell Lake Lodge

So …how would you like to spend the night atop the terminal moraine of an extinct Cascade glacier? Here's your chance to do so in relative luxury. The mountain of ice that scooped out Odell Lake bulldozed the rocks and dirt that make up the southeast side of the lake where Odell Lake Lodge now resides.

If Diamond Lake Resort can be described as the "Mother of all Mountain Lake Resorts," Odell Lake Lodge would be the friendly Grandfather Resort. Founded in 1902, this is apparently **the oldest of the mountain lake resorts in Oregon.** Located on the east end of Odell Lake where Odell Creek begins, the dog friendly resort offers cabins for rent year-round.

During the winter, this is ground zero for the cross-country ski crowd with many miles of trails at your doorstep. Skis, snowshoes and sleds are available for rent after the snow flies. The marina has moorage and offers boats for rent. The lodge has a restaurant (that serves excellent food) and an attractive patio overlooking the creek and the marina. On summer weekends, the lodge hosts live music on the patio next to the outdoor fireplace.

The cabins are on the glacial ridge above the lake, many with magnificent views. For those seeking peace and quiet, request cabin 17, the one at the end of the resort road. Contact Odell Lake Lodge at 541-433-2540.

## Campgrounds in the Odell Lake Area:

### Odell Creek Campground

Located on the east end of the lake adjacent to Odell Lake Lodge, Odell Creek Campground has 30 fee sites with several waterfront. A few of the camp sites are located on two small peninsulas with water on virtually three sides. There's a boat launch and drinking water available and with the resort so close, a restaurant and store too!

### Sunset Cove Campground

This camp is located on the south side of Highway 58 amid the towering trees. There's a boat launch at adjacent Chinquapin Point with a fish cleaning station.

The day-use area is promoted as a place for the wind surfing crowd, separate from the boat launch. It's $5 to use the day-use area. Sunset has 24 fee sites and wheelchair accessible facilities.

## Princess Creek Campground

Located on the north side of Odell Lake with big views to the south of Diamond Peak, Princess Creek has two docks adjacent to the boat launch.

The campground has water, handicap accessible toilets, and 46 fee sites, some which can accommodate trailers to 50 feet.

The large day-use area is east of the boat landing with a sunny southern exposure. This is another beach where the wind is reliable in the afternoons and wind jockeys can show off their stuff.

*Early morning calm near Princess Creek turns big Odell Lake into a giant mirror.*

## Willamette Pass

Back on Highway 58 heading west we soon come to the West Lake Access Road (the road to Shelter Cove Resort), The Pacific Crest Trail, the Willamette Pass Ski Area and the beginning of a new adventure exploring Northern Oregon.

It's with much sadness (I'm wiping a tear from my eye right now), that we part ways here, I've really enjoyed taking the drive with you. It doesn't mean we have to break-up forever though, buy my other book, **A Twisting Journey Continues**!

See you on the trail!

~ Ed W. McBee

# Join Us on a Romp through Northern Oregon!

The Oregon section of the Pacific Crest Trail ends in the north at the Columbia River. Hikers on the PCT walk across the river on The Bridge of the Gods at the town of Cascade Locks and enter the state of Washington.

Following the PCT to The Bridge of the Gods, the companion book to this volume titled *A Twisting Journey Continues, Northern Oregon Backroads Guide to the PCT* winds its high country way from Willamette Pass to the Columbia River.

Find that book or this one online, at **OregonBackroads.com** or at your friendly independent book dealer.

**See you on the trail in northern Oregon!**

# PLACES, NAMES AND PLANTS INDEX

## A

American Avocets  97
American White Pelican  82
Anderson Springs  122
Annie Creek  114
Annie Spring Entrance Station  117
Applegate Lake  37
Applegate Peak  120
Applegate River  22, 30, 33, 36, 37
Applegate Trail  62, 74
Applegate Valley  32, 33
Ashland  21, 40, 61, 64–73
Ashland Creek  64–65, 72
Aspen Inn Motel  109
Aspen Point Campground  88

## B

Barlow Toll Road  164
Barron's Station  57, 62
Bashō, Matsuo  143
Beaver Creek Road  21, 25, 35, 36
Bella Union  31
Benchmark Maps  13, 69, 106, 147
Big Draw Creek  86
Big Draw Road. *See* Forest Road 2520
Big Red Mountain  46–47
Big Spring  86
Birds Point Road  141, 145, 150
Bloomsbury Books  71
Blue Ledge Mine  35
Boomtown Saloon  23, 32
Bridge of the Gods  186

Britt Musical Festival (Brittfest)  28–29
Britt, Peter  28–29, 32
Britt Trails  32
Broken Arrow Campground  133
Brown Mountain  87, 88
Buckhorn Road  68, 73, 75
Buckhorn Springs Retreat Center  74
Bunker Hill Campground  154

## C

Calapooya Divide  145, 160, 162
Calapooya Gap  161, 162
Calapooya Mountains  146, 162, 166–167
California Tortoiseshell butterfly  161
Callahan's Lodge  22, 60–61
Cascade Locks  186
Cascade Mountains  10, 69, 71, 75, 78, 86, 89, 92, 148
Cascade-Siskiyou National Monument  78
Castle Rock Overlook  124
Central Oregon Military Road  171
Chiloquin  109
Chinquapin Point  183
Chinquapin tree  80
Clampers  57
Clarke, Clinton C.  6
Clearwater Falls  135–136
Clearwater River  136, 195
Cleetwood Cove  115, 125–126
Cloudcap Overlook  115, 124
Colestin Road  54, 57, 59

Colestin Valley  52
Columbia River  6, 11, 186
Contorta Point Campground  177
Copper Butte  37
Cornett Lake  174
Cow Creek Glade  39, 42–43, 49
Cowhorn Mountain  145, 162, 167, 176
Crater Lake  vi, 6, 29, 68, 86, 91, 92, 106, 107, 109, 112–119, 127, 150
Crater Lake Lodge  107, 116, 118, 127
Crater Lake National Park  vi, 106, 107, 109, 112–117
Crescent Creek  175, 180
Crescent Creek Cottages  180
Crescent Lake Campground  177
Crescent Lake Junction  146, 158, 159, 179–181
Crescent Lake Resort  175, 176
Crescent Ranger Station  147
Crystal Creek  95
Crystal Springs  155
Crystal Springs Recreation Site  99–100

## D

Dead Indian Memorial Road  67, 68, 73, 85, 86, 92
Deadman's Curve  36
Dellenback Bike Trail  130
Deschutes National Forest  147, 168
Deschutes River  168
Diamond Lake  vi, 105, 106, 107, 129–132, 148, 167
    Café  132
    Campground  133

    Corrals  133
    Gas Station  93, 134
    Ranger District  147
    Resort  128, 132
Diamond Peak Wilderness  173, 177, 179
Donomore Creek  41
Donomore Meadows  22, 41
Doppler radar (Mount Ashland)  51
Douglas County  168
Dread and Terror  152
Dutchman Peak  39, 45
Dutchman Peak Lookout  18, 22, 36, 38, 42
Dutton Ridge  120

## E

East Access Road  181
East Lemolo Campground  154
East Rim Road  107, 115, 119
E Clampus Vitas  57
Elliot Creek  37
Emigrant Creek  74
Emigrant Lake Park  63, 73
Emigrant Pass  171

## F

Farrell Lake  173, 174
Fawn Lake  177
Fish Lake Resort  68, 91
Forest Park Trails (Jacksonville)  31
Forrester Pass  6
Fort Klamath, Historic  110
Fort Klamath Town  109, 114
Free Emigrant Road  164

## G

Grayback Road  117, 122
Great Meadow  92
Green Springs Inn  68, 77, 78
Green Springs Summit  21, 22, 63
Griffin Pass  67, 69, 84–87
Grouse Gap  22, 47, 49–51
    Shelter  50

## H

Harriman Springs Resort  94
High Lakes Trail  88
Hillman Peak  121
Hobart Bluff  75
Hornbrook Formation  73
Howard Prairie Dam Road  67, 82, 83
Howard Prairie Lake  69, 82
    Recreation Area  82
    Resort  82
Howard Prairie Recreation Area  68
Hudson's Bay Company  57
Hyatt Lake  80
    Campground  80–81
    Resort  81

## I

Iditarod  100
Indigo Lake  166, 167
Inlet Campground  141, 154, 155
Interstate 5  8, 20, 22, 25, 47, 52, 59

## J

Jackson County Park  22
Jackson Creek  32
Jackson Gap  22, 25, 38, 39, 42, 43, 45
Jacksonville  23–32
Jacksonville Barber Shop  30
Jacksonville Hill  32
Jacksonville Inn  32
Jeffrey Pine  85
Jeffrey's Shooting Star  156
Jo's Motel  101, 109
June Lake  166, 167

## K

Keene Creek  78, 79
Kelsay Horse Camp  152
Keno Access Road  67, 83–85
Kerr Notch  121
Kimball State Park  104, 105, 112, 113
Klamath
    Birding Trail  100
    County  86
    Falls  77, 93
    Lake  69, 90, 92, 93, 95–98
    Mountains  78
Klamath Basin  109, 110, 120
Klamath Basin National Wildlife
    Refuge  98
Klum Landing Campground  83
Kokanee  150, 154

## L

Lake Charline  160
Lake Creek  130
Lake in Legend Overlook  125
Lake of the Woods  87
    Resort  67
    Resort Road  67, 86
Lake Timpanogas. *See* Timpanogas
    Lake

Las Palmas, Jacksonville  32
Lazuli bunting  47
Lemolo Falls  135, 151
   Trail  150
Lemolo Lake  135, 150
   Intersection  105, 134, 141
   Resort  105, 135, 141
Lemolo Lake, Campgrounds at  154, 156
Lemolo Lake General Store  149
Linda Lake  145, 155, 156, 160
   Campground  160
Lithia Park  64–65, 72
Little Applegate River  33, 47
Little Deschutes River  175
Little Hyatt Lake  67, 79
Little Hyatt Road  67, 73, 77, 79
Lodgepole pine  177
Long John Saddle  44, 46–48
Lost Creek Campground  117, 122
Lost Wagon Train  163, 164, 171
Louie's Bar and Grill  71
Lovett, Lyle  19

## M

Maidu Lake  152
Malone Springs  98, 99
   Boat launch  98
   Campground  98
Manley's Tavern  180
Marley, Bob  1
Mazama Village  117
McKee Covered Bridge  25, 35
McLeod, Alexander  57
Medford  28, 128

Meridian Overlook  21, 48–49
Middle Fork Willamette River  160, 163–166
Modoc Indian War  110
Mormon Fritillary butterfly  170
Mountain bluebird  47
Mountain House Kitchen  179
Mountain Lakes Wilderness  88
Mount Ashland  42, 43, 52, 54
   Campground  51
   Ski area  52, 53
   Ski Road (1151)  21, 25
   Summit Road  22, 51, 52
Mount Bailey  128–133
   Trail  132
Mount Everest  4
Mount Hood  6, 164
Mount Mazama  112, 120, 123–125
Mount McLoughlin  48
Mount Scott  120, 125, 126
   Trailhead  125
Mount Shasta  15, 42, 49, 51, 53
Mount Thielsen  120, 127, 130, 134
   Viewpoint  128
   Wilderness  152
Mustard Seed Cafe, Jacksonville  32

## N

Nicholson Road  67, 101
North Entrance Station  116, 128
North Junction  116, 127
North Umpqua River  139, 140
North Umpqua Trail  150, 152

## O

Oakridge  167, 169

Ranger Station  147
Observation Gap  43
Observation Peak  38, 42, 43
   Botanical Area. *See* Cow Creek Glade
Odell Creek  183
   Campground  181
Odell Lake  145, 146, 181–184
   Lodge  181, 183
Odell Sportsman Center  180
Odessa  93
Ogden, Peter Skeine  57
Old Baldy Peak  86
Oldenburg Lake trail  158
Old Highway 99  21, 57, 60–62, 73
Ollalie Lake Scenic  11
Opal Lake  145, 164
   Trailhead  168
Oregon City  164
Oregon Shakespeare Festival  71
Osprey  81
Osprey Viewing Area  82

## P

Pacific Corp  139, 143, 147, 155
Pacific Crest Trail Association (PCTA)  4, 6
Pacific Crest Trail (PCT)  2, 3, 6–8, 10, 71, 79, 85, 86
Pederson Sno-Park  68, 86
Pelican Butte  92, 120
Petty, Tom  103
Phantom Ship  119, 120
   Overlook  121
Pilot Rock  52, 53, 75

Pinnacles  115, 123
   Overlook Trailhead  121
   Road  105, 119–122
Plaikni Falls  121–122
Point Comfort Lodge  94
Poole Creek Campground  141, 147
Princess Creek Campground  184
Pumice Castle Overlook  124
Pumice Desert  128
Pussypaw  174

## R

Rainbow Bay Picnic Area  88
Red Buttes Wilderness  33, 37
Red Cone  128
Red Rocks  83
Rocky Point  92
   Boat Launch  95, 98
   Resort  90, 95, 96, 97
   Road  67, 93
Rogue River  26, 28, 57, 69, 106
   National Forest  36, 69
   Wars  57
Ruch  21, 25, 32–33

## S

Sand Creek  122
Sand Hill Crane  82, 97
Sandy River  164
Sawtooth Mountain  160, 166–167
Secret Swimming Hole  83, 84
Shelter Cove Resort  181, 184
Silver Fork Gap  21, 25, 27, 36–39, 45
Silvery Blue butterfly  26
Simax Beach Day-Use Area  179

Simax Group Campground  179
Siskiyou Crest  45, 48, 53, 57
Siskiyou Gap  47
Siskiyou Mountains  20, 22, 28, 33, 35, 39, 45, 49, 59, 61, 62
Siskiyou Peak/Trail  44, 48–49
Siskiyou Summit  22, 52, 59, 61
Sky Lakes Wilderness  86–87
Skyline Trail  6
Skyrocket Gilia  46
Snell Lake  173
Soda Mountain Wilderness  69, 74, 78
South Shore Day-Use Area  133
Spring Campground  177
Spring River  154, 155
Standing Stone Brewery and Restaurant  71
Star Ranger Station  24, 26, 35
Start O' Willamette Trail  166
Steel Visitor Center  116–118
Stevens Pass  3
Summit Creek  171, 173
Summit Lake  171–173
  Campground  171
Sun Notch  119, 120
Sun Pass Ranch  109
Sunset Campground  88

# T

Talent  47
Tandy Bay Day-Use Area  175
Thielsen View Campground  134
Timpanogas Lake  141, 155
  Campground  166

Shelter  167
Tokatee Falls  135, 139
Tranquil Cove Day-Use Area  175–176
Trapper Creek  181
Trinity Alps  42, 49
Tunnel 13  59
Tyler Creek Road  74

# U

Umpqua
  Hot Springs  152
  National Forest  106, 132, 147
  River  139, 140, 151, 162
Union Peak  120
United States Hotel  32
Upper Applegate River Road  22, 33
Upper Klamath Basin  95, 101
Upper Klamath Lake  69, 90, 97, 98
  Canoe Trail  95

# V

Valley View Winery  33, 34
Vidae Falls  118, 119
Vidae Ridge  120

# W

Warm Spring Creek Falls  152–153
Washington State  3, 11, 59
Watchman Peak  121
Water Ouzel  36
Watson Falls  137, 138
West Rim Road  116
Westside Road  91–93, 99, 101
Whitebark pine  124, 127

Whitebark Pine Picnic Area  125
Whitefish Creek Trail  179
Whitefish Horse Camp  179
Whitehorse Falls  136
White Mule Trail  152
Wildcat Campground  81
Willamette
 Inn  180
 Pass  v, 8, 144, 146, 167, 181, 184
 River  162, 163
 Valley  164, 171
Willow Point Campground  83
Windigo Pass  146, 152, 156, 158
Windigo Pass Road (Forest Rd 60)  145, 156, 158
Windy Group Campground  179
Windy Pass Trail  167
Winema National Forest  69, 86, 101
Wizard Island  121, 126, 127
Woodrat Mountain  32
Wood River  108, 111–113
 Day-Use Area  104, 105, 111
 Loop  104, 109, 110
 Springs  112
Wrangle Camp  46
Wrangle Gap  21, 40, 43, 45–47

# Y

Yurts  177–178

# ROAD INDEX

## Forest Roads

**20 Road** (Siskiyou Crest Road)  20, 21, 22, 25, 36–38, 40, 44–53

**40S01 Road**  25, 40–43

**60 Road** (Windigo Pass Road)  145, 155–160

**362 Road**  163

**680 Road** (Warm Spring Creek Falls Trailhead)  152

**700 Road**  145, 155, 156, 160

**740 Road**  160

**770 Road**  160–162

**800 Road**  45, 151

**840 Road** (Lemolo Falls Trailhead)  141, 151

**2025 Road** (Silver Fork Gap)  22, 25, 37, 38, 40–42

**2154 Road**  145, 160–164, 168, 169

**2520 Road** (Big Draw Road)  84, 85

**2610 Road** (Birds Point Road)  105, 141, 145, 150, 152

**2612 Road**  152, 155–159

**3100 Road** (NF 33)  67, 99, 101

**3401 Road**  141, 151

**6010 Road** (Summit Lake to Crescent Lake)  144–146, 167, 169, 173, 174

## Oregon State Highways

**Hwy 58**  145, 158, 167, 169, 180, 181, 184

**Hwy 62**  104, 105, 106, 109, 114

**Hwy 66**  21, 25, 53, 61, 63

**Hwy 99**  (See Old Highway 99)

**Hwy 138**  105, 106, 127, 128, 134–136

**Hwy 140**  66–68, 86, 91, 92

**Hwy 230**  105, 128, 130

**Hwy 238**  21, 25, 32, 33

*Showy Bunchberry Dogwood (cornus canadensis) is commonly found in the moist woods of stream side environments. I found this one next to the Clearwater River. After pollination the plant produces tightly clustered bunches of bright red berries*

**For more info about Ed McBee's backroads guides please visit:**

**www.OregonBackroads.com**

www.ingramcontent.com/pod-product-compliance
Lightning Source LLC
Chambersburg PA
CBHW051546010526
44118CB00022B/2593